THE
BLUFFER'S® GUIDE
TO
MEN & WOMEN

ANTONY MASON
MARINA MURATORE

GW00601189

Oval Books

Published by Oval Books
335 Kennington Road
London SE11 4QE
United Kingdom

Telephone: +44 (0)20 7582 7123
Fax: +44 (0)20 7582 1022
E-mail: info@ovalbooks.com
Web site: www.ovalbooks.com

The Bluffer's® Guide to Men, and
The Bluffer's® Guide to Women
first published as one volume 2004

Series Editor – Anne Tauté

Cover designer – Rob Oliver
Cover image – Rob Gage/Getty Images
Printer – Cox & Wyman Ltd.
Producer – Oval Projects Ltd.

The Bluffer's® Guides series is based
on an original idea by Peter Wolfe.

For their invaluable contributions to these guides
acknowledgement and thanks are given to:
Drew Launay, Nick Yapp, Mark Mason,
Cathy Douglas, Sally Horton, Eva Lipniaka,
Catriona Scott, Pauline Rozendaal, Jill Howell,
and the originators of the points given on
pages 62 and 123.

ISBN-13: 978-1-903096-30-8
ISBN-10: 1-903096-30-8

MEN

CONTENTS

THE KEY TO UNDERSTANDING WHAT MEN ARE ABOUT

What are men about? This is a question that has perplexed women since the first Neanderthal beefcake dragged a carcass into the cave with a hopeful grin all over his face. It is also the question that men ask today, struggling to wipe that same grin off their faces as they return from the supermarket minus several key items.

For five million years, science has been unable to answer the question. But where science fails, you, the bluffer, can succeed. A lofty ambition, you might suppose. But it is precisely because men have avoided analysis, that the smallest insight will instantly single you out as an expert. By absorbing what is contained in the following pages, and deploying it whenever the subject of men crops up in conversation (a far from rare event), you will gain the status of one who thoroughly understands the less fair sex.

A useful starting thesis is that men are about not failing. Their entire life is devoted to avoiding failure. Whatever it costs, whatever mental gymnastics are required, however strong the evidence to the contrary, men vehemently assert that they do not fail – in anything. They are great lovers, superlative wits, amazing drinkers, fantastic technicians, brilliant lateral thinkers, unbeatable sportsmen and undeniably clever at anything else that may be required of them. Therefore, they are indispensable to women, who have difficulties in all these fields.

To preserve this self-deception, men have to believe that there is more to them than there really is. Deep down they know they have not progressed mentally since the age of 15. All that has changed in adulthood is the type and extent of the mess and damage they leave behind them. They have abandoned their childhood toys for mobile phones, car stereo systems, the Internet, real guns, the Stock Market and women.

But, whatever men know deep down, they want women to believe that men are superior, so superior that they can laugh at the slogan that reads: 'Women like the simple things in life, like men.' It's a joke almost worthy of a man.

FUNDAMENTAL DIFFERENCES

For decades, scientists, social reformers, and feminists have been arguing that men are pretty much the same as women. Men themselves, however, have tended to disagree, basing their opinion on the blindingly obvious (always their preferred method). The empirical observation of any adolescent boy in mirror sunglasses, groping his way along a nudist beach, is that men and women are manifestly not the same at all. And nor are their responses to one another.

We recommend that you tend towards this latter view. The retreat from hardcore 1970s feminism is in your favour: it is once more permissible to state openly, and in mixed company, that men and women are really quite different. However, your watchword in this argument should be moderation: gender stereotypes may be less extreme, subtler, and more diluted than in previous generations, but the sentiments expressed by this popular bumper sticker still prevail: 'Women who seek to be equal to men lack ambition.'

In other words, these days men can get away with less.

Brawn

Men are built differently from women, which they are very happy to demonstrate at the drop of a hat, or any other item of clothing. They are also built differently from each other, though here it is usually a matter of quantity rather than quality.

There are several handy facts to keep at the ready as you go about your bluffing. (N.B. They are based on the average or mean, rather than the magnificent):

- Male babies are born bigger than female babies.

- Men are stronger than women. Nearly twice as much of their body is devoted to muscle tissue (average 57 lbs, compared to 33 lbs).

- Men are 10% heavier and 7% taller than women.

- Men's main internal organs (heart, lungs, kidneys, waste-disposal units) are larger, and their bone structure is more massive.

- Men's brains are bigger, by about 5 oz (the weight of a generous apple), which is why they find using the whole brain at any one time more exhausting.

- Men can also run faster. They don't have airbags in the front seat.

There are physiological reasons for these differences. Men can run faster because their bodies contain a higher concentration of haemoglobin which carries oxygen in the blood, and the greater the concentration, the more quickly oxygen can be taken up in an active body. Men also run faster because they have a narrower pelvis, which means that when running they need to rotate it less fast than women in proportion to the distance covered. It also means that no man can walk like Marilyn Monroe.

We suggest, however, that you steer conversation away from the physical differences between men and women. They do not explain why men behave differently. The caveman analogy comes in handy at this point – and few men will take offence. Most will happily identify with cavemen, and rather wish they could be cavemen again, back in the days when things were much simpler.

In those days, B.C. (Before Contraception), women spent the greater part of their lives pregnant and child-rearing, and could not stray far from the cave. Men roamed around in packs, hunting wild animals for food and looking for trouble. They had to be physically tough to outwit their prey, and rivals who wanted access to their cave and their women. One should be careful not to make all this seem too idyllic.

Since early man bothered little with etiquette, it is likely that he feasted on mammoth rump steak, while early woman had to be content with chewing the hide. So man grew stronger, and woman grew weaker.

This basic modus vivendi took several million years to develop. You can point out that it hasn't evolved any further in the intervening aeons. In any case, modern culture still reinforces this attitude: men, rather than women, are the ones expected to fight wars, play rough sports and hit the burglar over the head with the poker.

There are plenty of vestiges of the caveman in modern man, and this is not just in his attitude to women. Men like to show off, beating their chests and hollering to demonstrate who dominates, and who has something to prove, before phoning their wife with what they hope will be a believable excuse for not coming home.

Brain

Research into the brain reinforces the historical divergences between the sexes. These have been refined and honed over countless generations; those men not blessed with certain vital skills – or virtues – would not have lived long enough to reproduce and pass them on. It has been found that:

- men have greater spatial aptitudes: originally necessary for following bison over the grasslands, today evident in better map-reading skills and sense of orientation. In laboratory studies, men score over women in tests involving mazes and perspective – but then, so do rats.

- men have more precise target-directed motor skills, once vital for aiming javelins at mammoths from 100 paces, now displayed by a greater skill at reversing cars into small spaces, zapping warlords on play stations and throwing darts in the pub. Almost every game or sport played in the world today has been invented to emphasise male superiority, with the exception of synchronised swimming.

- in good light, men can pick out smaller objects in the distance, especially if they are moving – useful for bringing home the prime ingredients for hedgehog pie and avoiding police speedtraps.

- men can tolerate twice as much noise as women, and that is not just because they are making it.

It is generally, though grudgingly, agreed by men that women have the advantage with social skills and language. This is because of women's greater activity between the two hemispheres of the brain, and a larger concentration of cells in the region of the cortices associated with languages and listening.

11

If you wish to strike a contradictory note on this topic, offer the opinion that the lack of cross-currents between the hemispheres in men's brains may be to men's advantage. Poorer communication skills and a less developed sense of empathy help them to be more single-minded and more focused, and better suited to waging war and stripping lead off roofs, where being overly concerned about the consequences could be a distinct disadvantage.

Blame Testosterone

Virtually everyone – including men – agrees that men could behave better. Few, however, know the scientific basis for men's transgressions, so this is fertile ground for the bluffer. You can safely put your eggs in one basket: testosterone.

Testosterone is the male hormone produced by the testicles, and accounts for the development of the male sex organs in the womb and their subsequent development at puberty. The rest of the tale hangs from there, as it were.

Testosterone makes men masculine. It gives them:

- a deeper voice
- more body hair
- virility
- aggression
- that oddly gamey whiff to be savoured in any locker room – one that is not related to sweaty trainers.

Testosterone helps to create the distinctively male brain. It affects the way the body reacts to stress and copes with adrenaline. Bristling with testosterone, men look for scary and exciting experiences, such as hurling themselves off heights on the end of elastic bands, kerb-crawling, and eating the hottest possible curry. Testosterone impels men to take risks. Men see this as a point in their favour since it makes them more predisposed than women to take up challenges, to clinch that billion-dollar deal, to reach the top of Mount Everest, to cross the Atlantic in a sieve, to make a pass at their best friend's wife. Unfortunately it also leads them into trouble. Men are more accident-prone than women; in fact, they are four times more likely to die in an accident.

Men's ability to judge distances when at the wheel, and to assess accurately the gaps between oncoming vehicles explains why men think they are better drivers than women. Paradoxically, because they think they are better drivers, and enjoy the testosterone-induced thrill of speed, they also drive faster. Insurance statistics show that 94% of serious accidents are caused by men.

Nowadays, testosterone is blamed for all manly misdeeds. Men are not entirely comfortable with this. It suggests they aren't responsible for their actions, which is how they prefer to view women – i.e., if any-one is hopelessly adrift in a sea of hormones, it is women, not men. Should you find yourself bluffing to such an intransigent male, silence him with the fact, incontrovertible even to men, that it is they who are responsible for the vast proportion of violent crime. When men are in their late teens and early twenties testosterone levels reach their peak, aggression comes to the fore and, for some, beating up rival foot-ball fans can be more thrilling than kicking the ball into a net.

Research among male football supporters shows that watching their team win can produce a 20% increase in testosterone levels, and that they will experience a testosterone surge merely by *thinking* about their team's forthcoming fixtures.

Both men and women possess varying amounts of testosterone and oestrogen. Medical tests carried out on violent women in U.S. jails show that they have higher than average levels of testosterone, another statistic to give the male hormone a bad name.

However, one advantage of testosterone, as any school teacher will tell you, is that it makes boys and men less susceptible to infestations of head lice.

GROWING UP

Men don't grow up if they can possibly help it. The majority have to, however, and during this process suffer the following four stages:

Boys Will Be Boys

Boys become boys in the seventh week of pregnancy. At a critical moment, the vital 'Y' element of the male XY sex chromosome triggers a conversion process: the potentially female attributes of the foetus atrophy, the penis and the testes develop, and testosterone goes into full production.

If your taste is for high-risk bluffing, you may care to posit the argument that this detonation by the Y chromosome represents a positive act of divergence from the prototype; it suggests innate male dynamism, perhaps even superiority. But beware: you lay yourself open to the observation that it could also explain why there are more male transvestites than female – men have more female in them than women have male. We advise you to stick to research which indicates that boys show innately masculine behaviour when still in the womb. While female foetuses tend to move their lips, rehearsing their well-known talent for talk, unborn boys thrash their limbs about pretending to be astronauts in their own little private space capsule.

In the nursery and the playground, boys demonstrate early their propensity for noisy, rough-and-tumble, high-energy games. This is transmuted in later life to body-contact team sports. Boys pit themselves against each other with boxing, batting, and balls. They become expert at creating noise and making big expansive movements – imitating the sound of machine-gun fire as they fly hand-held plastic fighter planes around the garden in a dogfight with the cat.

Whereas girls will play quietly for hours with a toy put in front of them, boys will want to investigate everything in sight. But their innate inner drive dictates that they will soon be distracted and move on to something else. In later life this frequently takes a female form.

In one test arranged by sociologists, girls and boys were offered dolls to play with. The girls cuddled and talked to the dolls: the boys took their clothes off.

Teenage Man

All teenagers are misunderstood by adults, but male teenagers are misunderstood by female teenagers as well, and female teenagers are what matter to them most. The only time in his life that the male really tries to understand the female is when he is a teenager. After that, he will have had such a rough time being teased, taunted, unnerved and rejected, he may give up for ever. As far as men are concerned, teenage girls can be held totally responsible for men's eventual adult behaviour.

Middle-Age Man

The seven-year itch, the eleven-year itch, and the mid-life crisis all occur between the mid-thirties and late forties. Thirty-nine is the worst age of all, when a man takes stock of what he has or has not achieved before being inevitably launched into the Over Forties. It is at about this time in his life that he gets bored with his job and worries that he is no longer attractive. ('I'm losing hair off my head', cries the anguished hero of *City Slickers*, 'and starting to get it in my ears and on my back. I'm starting to look like *The Fly*!') Middle-age man tries to reassure himself by flirting with secretaries and air stewardesses, is desperate if he fails and even more desperate if he succeeds because he is not at all ready to cope with the ensuing marital problems.

On the plus side, he is probably better off than ever, more self-assured, more confident, better at sex, and often, as a result, quite unbearable.

Dirty Old Man

Though men have the advantage over women of being thought to get more attractive as they get older, old men become grumpy. This is apparently the effect of the gradual decrease in testosterone level, but it is also a by-product of the fact that all those urges and ambitions that once motivated them suddenly seem rather pointless.

Younger men are encouraged by the sight of old men marrying young women and siring children when well into their nineties: it gives them some hope of distant adventures. They are not aware of the effort this involves, nor the failure rate.

Men lose their fertility at a rate of about 12% per annum (cumulative, or index linked) from the age of

30. Testosterone diminishes with age, and with it goes not only their libido but also their sparkle. In the U.S., men anxious to avoid the embarrassment of impotence on a date have found it useful to stick a testosterone patch, similar to the smokers' nicotine patch, to remote parts of their anatomy. Neither party feels very flattered if this is discovered.

SEX

'A very marked difference between the sexes,' noted diarist Elizabeth Delafield in the 1930s, 'is the male tendency to procrastinate everything in the world except sitting down to a meal and going up to bed.' This is a chivalrous observation befitting its date. In reality, most men would unhesitatingly scrub round the meal if bed was in the offing.

Men are said to think of sex every six minutes – unless they are actually having sex, when to delay the final surge they think about real ale, the nine times table, or reinforced concrete construction.

After thinking about sex every six minutes for six days, men are beginning to need to do something about it. Any longer and they become like a bull elephant in musk – agitated, consumed by forces they only vaguely comprehend. They are often intensely grateful to women who take pity, and help them out. Few men can summon the objectivity of a committed misogynist, who complained of sex: 'the pleasure is momentary, the position ridiculous and the expense damnable.'

Men will do anything for sex, and will behave quite out of character to achieve it, such as spending several hours being romantic, and paying attention to what a woman says. A woman can probably persuade a man to undertake any favour against the promise of sex: put up a curtain rail, iron a shirt, ring the dentist...

Bluffing is often at its most effective when arguing against a received wisdom. If you know enough to achieve this, your audience will think, you really must be in command of the subject. Accordingly, we counsel you to dismiss the 'men thinking with their testosterone is bad' thesis. Opine that men are simply the vehicles for the human urge to regenerate. Suggest that this is a bit of a burden, and given that sperm are produced from puberty onwards, something of a life sentence. Thus, since most men would happily cast their seed far and wide given half a chance, monogamy represents a serious sacrifice. It is said that in denying himself sex outside marriage, a man makes a biological sacrifice comparable to women having children.

Men are controlled and regulated by their sperm – masses of them clamouring to get out and reproduce at the earliest possible opportunity. Some 100 million are released on each ejaculation and only one is needed for successful fertilisation. Men never do things by halves.

Selfish Genes

Sperm are not overly fussy about how and when they get launched on their mission. Men can do the necessary in just about any circumstance you care to think of – except, perhaps, in front of a critical audience. However, the genes get a say in this.

Genes seem to have preferences – a phenomenon expressed as 'selfish'. Their agenda is to find the best partner with which to reproduce and ensure their survival. Men project the genes' preference, or the sexual urge, into women – metaphorically as well as literally. They have ways of verbalising the genes' preferences in such expressions as 'fwaw!', 'cor!', 'she's gorgeous'. This urge is sometimes called the 'genetic imperative'– a useful term to explain just about anything a man thinks or does.

It does not quite stop with sex. If it did, men would be concerned only with impregnating as many women as possible. What restrains them (most of them, anyhow) is the need to know that their offspring can be nurtured long enough to ensure a subsequent generation. Men may attempt to dress up their behaviour in any number of ways, but it always comes back to the genes. Never fear that your male bluffees will take offence at this analysis. Few, in fact, will object. It relieves them of responsibility. They can look dispassionately upon the swelling evidence of their uncontrollable urges as an alien force, hold up their hands and declare with a shrug: 'Nothing to do with me.'

Virginity

Peer group pressure makes virginity a burden and an embarrassment for men. For women there is at least some tradition of merit attached.

The difficulty is finding someone with whom to dispose of it. It's a tough one. On the one hand, an adolescent male will do all he can to make out that he is an experienced lover, and the lie increases with age. On the other, he is certain that his first proper sexual encounter will be such a tidal wave of sensual experience that he is bound to make a complete hash of it. He knows the mechanics – he has studied this at length, and rehearsed it repeatedly. But the details remain obscure, and there is no way of predicting the input of the opposite party. It is liable to be a disaster.

This should not, of course, matter at all. But male

pride comes into play here, of the obstinate and hard-boiled kind that is difficult to dislodge. Ideally the inexperienced male lover needs the reassurance of sympathy and patience, and preferably a sense of fun. Unfortunately, male talk and girls' teenage magazines suggest that no-one should be satisfied with anything less than sexual olympics and immediate multiple orgasms.

We cannot over-emphasise the need for tact when the conversation enters this territory. The odds are that at least one of the men you're addressing will have insecurities about his early sex life. Exacerbate these and you will antagonise him; an inconsiderate bluffer is a self-defeating bluffer. Gently throw in a mention of surveys which suggest that no less than 25%, if not 40% (truth is a victim here), of men entering university are virgins. And that roughly the same number are virgins when they leave.

It is easy enough to spot a virgin. Most men will talk frankly and honestly (male-speak for boasting) to other men about their sexual encounters. The virgin will remain quiet. Instruction isn't practice, and he just cannot confidently imagine what it is really like. His mind reels at the very idea, and he is not sure he has the vocabulary.

Young men dream of being shown the way to pleasure and bliss by an experienced older woman – just like *The Graduate*. As Mae West put it: 'Men like women with a past because they hope history will repeat itself.'

Equipment

From infancy, boys learn that their penis has a life of its own – activity associated with mysterious and pleasurable feelings. Dangling so prominently, it has a permanent presence, is readily to hand, and seldom out of the mind.

The penis is the male organ par excellence. Men are so obsessed by this possession that they regard it as a pet and converse with it. This no doubt explains why it has so many pet names (see Glossary).

When aroused, it is operated entirely by hydraulics, the effect of blood being pumped into it. With nerve endings concentrated near the tip, it is a strange combination of rubbery inertness and sensitivity.

Worshipped by Hindus as a 'lingam', or symbol of Shiva, and by the Romans who made a fertility symbol out of the enormously well-endowed god Priapus, it is disconcerting for men to discover that modern women are not so impressed by their pride and joy. Indeed, many of them find the penis absurd, hilarious, down-right ugly, and certainly over-ambitious. Ridicule is one way to ensure that it fails to rise to its proper function.

As for the accompanying accoutrements, the testicles, by contrast, are as fragile as egg shells. A sharp knock or tap can induce excruciating pain, even retching and vomiting, to a degree no woman can fully appreciate. Not for nothing have these been singled out as the male weak spot, conveniently located for kicking or kneeing. They represent a major design fault, or evidence that God is a woman.

Size
Most men are secretly concerned about the size of their appendage, especially in the years before it has been put to the test.

They are constantly told that size does not matter – 'It's not how big it is, it's what you do with it' – but it still bothers them. They hear worrying stories of some women who cannot be satisfied with anything less

21

than Michelangelo's David, full scale. On the other hand, those who conclude by furtive glances in communal showers that theirs is above average, can harbour fears that their car may be too big for the garage.

The relaxed penis can be any size, depending on the ambient temperature. Cold induces unflattering shrivelling: this is why, at nudist beaches, men walk quickly towards their towels after swimming.

In erect form, size averages out. By producing statistics here, you can significantly boost your image as an 'expert' on men. The figures are guaranteed to provoke lively (and in all probability ribald) discussion, and people tend to perceive a correlation (correctly or otherwise) between how much a teacher has entertained them and how much he or she knows. The average size of an erect penis in Europe, you can mention nonchalantly, is 6 inches; in Asia 5; and in Africa 7. Before anyone produces a ruler, you can remind your audience that the average duration of intercourse for an orang-utan is 15 minutes, with a penis of just 1½ inches*.

Masturbation

Just about every man masturbates, from about the age of 12 onwards. It is through 'playing with himself' that a boy will first discover erections and, by persistent stroking, one day or night the world will suddenly turn inside out, as an extraordinary, dynamic sensation fills his entire body and produces a mysterious dollop of goo. Nothing quite prepares a male for this moment, and he will probably remember the time and place of it for the rest of his life.

Boys and men will go on practising for the real

* In metric: 152 mm, 127 mm, 178 mm, 38 mm, respectively.

thing throughout adolescence and into adulthood. There is a physical need to discharge a build-up of sperm, which if not resolved will express itself as an involuntary 'wet dream' during sleep

Masturbation is often accompanied by a slight sense of guilt, as is any solitary indulgence. But no-one really believes it is a sin any more, makes you blind or that it can put spots on your upper arms. 'Don't knock it,' said Woody Allen in *Annie Hall*, 'it's sex with someone you love.'

Performance

Premature ejaculation is the great male fear. The trouble is that coming too soon is a fact of life. It is not sperms' duty to hang about, and they require a fair amount of training to induce them to delay. Surveys have revealed that 75% of men ejaculate within two minutes of penetration. Some even jump the starting gun.

As with virginity, you must take great care not to alienate insecure males among your listeners. We suggest that you take the pressure off them (as it were) by referring to the conflicting sexual demands placed on them by their partner. Women, and in particular young women, demand foreplay to stimulate arousal as they seek to find the best route to pleasure. But all the time foreplay is going on, the sperm are massing on the starting line. This mismatch requires negotiation, time and perseverance to resolve – not qualities readily associated with the quenching of mutual lust. Condoms are the silver lining to the dual clouds of infection and conception: they desensitise men, so women have a better prospect of increased duration.

There is only one thing more worrying for men than

coming too soon: total mechanical failure. This may be brought on by an attack of anxiety, fear of failure, an excess of Dutch courage, or the natural built-in obsolescence of age. The high statistical occurrence of 'erectile dysfunction' which is said to affect one in every two men aged 40-70, has been outed by the world-wide success of the stiffening drug Viagra, boosted by the advertisements of Brazilian football star Pele (born 1940) along with puns from the press about balls, and rising to the task of conquering the taboo.

For men, orgasm is the raison-d'être of sex. They assume therefore that this is also the case for women, and cannot quite believe that women can be satisfied with less. Mutual orgasm represents the zenith of male sexual ambition – not a bad goal to aim at, but in reality, a difficult one to score. As a butler prone to keyholes once put it, 'Gentlemen often have more enthusiasm than skill.'

Libido

All men are chancers: the male sexual drive is strong enough to lead even TV evangelists astray. Some 25% of married men have had at least one extramarital affair – and this figure is based on those who admit to it. There are also plenty who prefer to believe that sex without penetration does not count.

Women tend to leave their husbands for someone else because they have reached the end of their tether; marital love has keeled over and seems impervious to revival. Men, on the other hand, often see an affair as a bit of an adventure to spice up their lives, to shore up their flagging egos. It does not mean that their love for their wife has evaporated, just that it is not all-consuming. There is some spare capacity (all those sperms swarming for migration), and someone has come into their lives who can give them a home. They will often be happy to motor along like this until one or other woman decides she no longer wants a part-timer.

Until viruses received wide publicity, it was generally considered acceptable for men to sleep around, especially in their youth. But there was a downside to this licence to bonk. It meant that even very young men could never admit that they hadn't had experience of sex. And this has led to the curse of the Burden of Sexual Experience. All men have to pretend they are sexual rogues, and not just to each other.

Women are party to this dreadful deceit. A husband who is seen as reliably faithful may be seen as a little dull – possibly even unattractive. It used to be the case among the French bourgeoisie that a husband who did not have a mistress was something of a social embarrassment. However, rogue males do not want to be confronted by rogue females because:

- they are demoralized women who are more sexually experienced than they are. It can lead to comparisons, and all comparisons are odious.
- they want to control a woman's sexuality to avoid any suspicion that they may be raising someone else's progeny.
- they take a dim view of women who behave as badly as they do.

Pornography

Many women find pornography baffling. Men don't. For bluffers trying to account for this conundrum, there is an agreeably neat explanation: women are turned on by what is done to them, men are turned on by what they see. Almost all men enjoy eroticism, and always have. They fantasise about sex all the time, so it is not difficult to market fantasy to them.

They profess to find sex videos and magazines inspiring, exciting and a little daring – it's rather like the first time they use a grown-up swear word: they are aware that this is something powerful, but don't really understand what it means.

When pressed about their attitude to pornography, men wilt. They surrender the first untenable position (that pornography is art), and take up a second indefensible position (that pornography is just a bit of fun). From this point it's not long before they retreat to a third position (that it doesn't do any harm), and a fourth (well, yes, all right then, it's demeaning), and a fifth (look, can't we talk about something else?). It is not an heroic defence, and it's a tragic certainty that, with the publication of the next day's pin-up, the same men will repeat the whole process.

However, the publishers of images of women with ginormous breasts are peddling an ancient myth that men necessarily like that kind of thing. Women who are less well endowed can sleep easier on this one – and probably do.

Prostitution

Men are perfectly capable of regarding sex in a totally impersonal way, and keeping it in a different compartment from notions such as love, family, or fishing. It is this disposition that leads men to seek gratification from prostitutes. Some men will argue that prostitution serves a valid function. It is a therapy; it services a male need by means of a neutral commercial transaction, which would probably otherwise have to be satisfied by less willing partners elsewhere; and like so many illicit things, it is also fun.

For balanced bluffing, however, it's advisable that you mention some of the counter-arguments, such as health and safety, and terms of contract. But never redundancy payments.

FEELINGS

It is, of course, a cheap joke to suggest that the very idea of men's feelings is a contradiction in terms. Men do have feelings, and they are not just all over their body.

The trouble is they are brought up to deny feelings, to bury them, in non-Latin countries anyway. Parents and peers train them not to show emotion, so that when deeply moved, they will turn to something intensely distracting – like ping-pong, horseplay, or pot-holes. When the Japanese head of a collapsed business or the Australian Prime Minister breaks rank and bursts into tears, it becomes headline news. The upshot of such sublimation is that men are more likely than women to suffer depression and have a 400% higher suicide rate.

Approval

Men are suckers for approval. A nod and a smile go a long way to winning the male heart. They want to feel that women have noticed them and that women need them. Best of all would be if women admired them. They would also like to feel that women trusted them, but that's probably hoping for too much.

Men would be putty in women's hands if they were given the eye-sparkling, adoring look of Ingrid Bergman in *Casablanca*, or the eye-smouldering one of Lauren Bacall in *To Have and Have Not*, just before she says 'If you want anything, just whistle...' It is when they yearn for this approval that men are at their most dog-like and appealing.

It has been a source of much anguish to men that women have discovered how much men long to be admired. Traditionally it was all the other way round – women pined for men's attention, affection, adoration. Men galloped by, scarcely noticing them, unless they needed rescuing. Today, women seldom need rescuing and men have traded in their steeds. This is complete gender reversal. Jane Austen has been swapped for Jackie Collins, and men are left to create new roles for themselves. Men now have to work far harder to earn that treasured approval, making the best job of it they can, with inadequate props.

Independence

Men are admired if they are independent, competent, self-sufficient, and if they do not match up to this they feel something of a failure. Their sense of independence is an important factor in their relationships. Women are likely to define themselves in terms of their chosen loved one; men are apt to see their loved one as a partner who might be cherished, but who does not redefine them.

An interesting by-product of this is that men prefer to feel that they are paying their way in a relationship. This fact is of particular value to the bluffer as it is very simple to work into conversation in a restaurant or bar. Men have to feel competent, they have to be the provider. This is the hunter instinct, an old habit that is taking a long time to die. Funnily enough, women do not seem to mind this.

By contrast, house-husbands who stay at home while their wives go out to work are still very much in the minority. They are readily identifiable because they see themselves as unusual, look faintly bruised and typically make elaborate justifications – usually 'economic circumstances' – as to why they are not pursuing a more conventional career.

At all times men like keeping their options open. It is all part of their urgent need for independence and to be seen to be independent, even if it makes them seem obstinate and foolish. Press them too hard and they will feel their options closing down. It is a fatal error to box a man into a corner. But give him the opportunity to say no, and he is more likely to say yes.

Pride

Men like to be right. If they say they admire a woman with ideas, they mean a woman who shares their ideas. Women find it is often best to tell men that they are right, even if they patently are not: there is little value in arguing. (Overheard from a man, expressed with the greatest conviction: 'I *know* I'm right – and if I'm not, it's a mistake.')

By the same token, men do not like to be contradicted: it is an assault on their fragile integrity. They cannot bear to be thought ineffectual or inadequate, and will avoid any situation which insinuates that they need help. You can advance this theory by using an example that everyone will recognise: men hate having to ask for directions from strangers. They would rather drive around a city with a car full of scratchy children for hours, getting ever later for lunch, than wind down the window and ask the way.

It looks too much as if they don't know.

All men realise that this instinct is absurd, but male pride is stronger than reason.

Stubbornness

Bluffers are under some obligation to point out that it is quite wrong to think of men as stubborn. They are not stubborn, and there is absolutely no point in suggesting that they are.

Men pride themselves on being tolerant, flexible, accommodating and forgiving, especially towards women. Saying that they are stubborn, intransigent, obstinate, or downright impossible, is evidence of a clear and simple failure to appreciate the masculine virtues of self-assurance, confidence, decisiveness, persistence and dogged determination. The argument is cut and dried; the case is closed. Men are not stubborn, and there is no way anyone is going to shift them from that point of view.

Socialising Skills

You may, on the other hand, concede that men are less socially adept than women. Evidence comes not just from casual observation, but also from brain scans and genetic research.

It has been discovered that only females are born with a 'switched on' socialising gene. It seems that males are not born with any genetically inherited socialising skills at all; they have to learn them.

This means that men are less aware of other people's feelings, oblivious to the effects of their behaviour, and difficult to reason with when upset; less pleasant altogether than women, poor things.

Nor are they intuitive. Men don't even have enough intuition to realise how much intuition women have.

Men believe that when women complain, or talk about a problem, they are demanding that men do something about it. Women don't always want something done. Often they want sympathy and comfort. But men would need intuition to know that.

Before incorporating this topic into your bluffing, you must be warned that when confronted with these biological facts, men exhibit one of two responses:

1. Arrogance, since it gives them a cast-iron excuse for behaving as they do.

2. Pique, because it puts them on the defensive, and men do not like to be seen at a disadvantage, or lacking in anything, in any field, ever.

If you get the first response, sit back and laugh with the rest of the group. If you get the second, have a crumb of comfort ready to offer to the disconcerted man. Assure him that it is not the mother who passes on the socialising genes to her daughter, but the father.

Conversation

The average woman uses 10,000 words a day in speech; the average man finds 4,000 perfectly adequate. Around the house, men's conversation is especially economical, often reduced to grunts and utterances of one syllable. For them, telephone calls are for the transmission of information, not for gossiping or the exchange of confidences.

Men have one fear greater than being proved wrong: being thought weak. In conversation with women, they generally tell their listeners what they think they want to hear. Their conversational strategy is devised to disguise their vulnerability. This has an intimidating effect on them as well. Men with low self-esteem worry about why the world isn't revolving around them. Confident men cannot help thinking that it does.

The confident man can dominate the conversation at a dinner party, brag about his achievements, attempt to cap the last story, and steer the discussion. If he is in an ebullient mood, he expects everyone to follow suit. As a result there is a fair chance that the atmosphere will be combative, stimulating, enlightening and amusing.

It could also be a crashing bore. But men have the antidote to this. They don't listen. They are too busy thinking what they are going to say next. It can come as a complete surprise to them to find someone with something sufficiently interesting to say to interrupt their thought processes.

The corollary of this, which is that women are attracted to men who are good at listening, can be a very handy tool as you conduct your bluffing. If one of your male listeners is talking too much, slip into the conversation the fact that accomplished seducers cultivate the virtue of listening well. You will find that he pipes down after that.

Opinions

Men feel obliged to have an opinion about everything. Being asked for their opinion is the one thing they are guaranteed to hear.

Even if they don't have much of one, they will want to express it. In many, as soon as a thought pattern flows through their brain it will start heading for the mouth, and will pour forth without hindrance, and regardless of whether others are talking at the time. (Men are great interrupters – though they have cunningly created the belief that interrupting is a female trait.) Many have learnt to withstand this impulse, but any delay tends to result in an even weightier pronouncement when it is released.

Men's pride does not allow them to be less knowledgeable than women. They therefore go to great lengths to make sure that they are well versed in any subject which might come up during a party, conference, car journey, flight, picnic. They are incurable purchasers of reference books, dictionaries and encyclopædias. *The Bluffer's® Guides* were invented by a man.

Buddies

Male friendships are centred round activities. Not for them cosy, supportive gossiping simply because 'it's good to talk'. When buddies meet, even after an absence of ten years, they are more likely to talk about last night's television than the failed marriages, horrendous operations, bankruptcies or other tragedies that have struck since they were last together.

So their buddies are people with like-minded interests – sailing, golfing, gardening, drinking, bird-watching – people with whom they do things, rather than talk about them. They muddle along with these chums comfortably when their pursuits coincide. They may even end up with a deep bond but, on the whole, friendship is not a question of baring their souls.

Most men tend not to develop close friends after the formative years of their lives – notably university. They are just too busy, too active, too mobile, too tied up with their work to make the effort. Their social lives increasingly revolve around their wives' friends, and the husbands of their wives' friends. The result is that the majority tend to end up with the diminishing number of buddies they started with, and many end up with few buddies to speak of. Or to.

Chauvinism

Male Chauvinists like being called Male Chauvinists. They take it as a compliment, not an insult.

They may be an outrageous and unacceptable figure in the modern age, but they cannot be written off completely. To every male trying to soothe the screaming baby with a bottle of expressed milk comes that momentary flash of envy and doubt when he thinks that perhaps the Chauvinist has got things just about right: no principles, no conscience, no housework, no danger of disappointed expectations – and, believe it or not, no shortage of female admirers.

Commitment

Men find it hard to commit themselves to a relationship. Getting them to do so is like getting hold of the soap in the bath.

A sense of commitment to a partnership – or rather the lack thereof – is one factor you can safely cite as the key difference between men and women. For men the very idea of commitment is uncomfortable: 'to commit' after all is the same verb used of suicide, or being sent to an asylum. Marriage also goes by the unnerving term 'wedlock'.

'A man is incomplete until he has married. Then he is finished,' said Zsa-Zsa Gabor, after considerable research. Men harbour the distinct fear that marriage will change them. Women simply hope it will.

A key factor in persuading people of your expertise

is how much highly-charged debate you can engender. And few debates have a higher charge than those you will engender by stating that, like other primates, men are not essentially monogamous, and the chances are that they will not be able to satisfy their sexual drives in one relationship. Current divorce rates of one in three in the U.K. and one in two in the U.S. would seem to be evidence of this.

Monogamy presents men with a real problem. They believe there is something unnatural about it. Although it is practised by 90% of bird species, only 3% of mammals are monogamous – and men see themselves more as gorillas than mistle thrushes.

Since men like to keep their options open, they like to think that there are ways to preserve their independence, even in the heart of a happy marriage. 'The sea is like a wife,' runs an old northern Spanish saying, 'she entices you, draws you in, then kills you' – a little strong, but the Spanish love anything that promises death. Men do see marriage as an end as much as a beginning. They try to guard against this by secretly holding on to far more of their former single way of life than women do.

On the other hand, men also accept marriage as a sensible compromise with joys of its own. There are a number of pay-offs to long-term commitment, such as:

- domestic comfort
- a captive audience
- increased tax allowance
- better catering arrangements.

A married man envies the single man on Saturday nights, but not on Sunday morning.

ATTITUDES

To Women

Secretly, men think women are cleverer than they are, but convention does not allow them to admit it. In fact, men and women share the same average I.Q. When this was revealed to the world in 1912, the male world was publicly shocked, but privately greatly relieved – they had no idea they were that smart.

Surveys, always trusty and hard-working pixies for any bluffer, can be especially useful here. Tell your listeners that in surveys, men consistently overestimate their I.Q.s (knowing that they are doing so), while women underestimate theirs (not knowing that they are doing so). Among couples, despite huge evidence to the contrary, the majority of women will state that their partner is the more intelligent of the two, and children of either sex will tend to say their father is more intelligent than their mother.

One of the smarter members of your audience may suggest that one interpretation of this is that more intelligent women do not have husbands, or partners or children. You must be prepared for this. Answer that the statistics do not support that reckoning – even though, you can add with a professorial air, there are 105 women to every 100 men in the Western world. The clue to the riddle, you can reveal, lies in the word 'intelligent': women are happy to settle for being considered equally capable. They know that most men are daunted by intelligent women, and to accommodate this, deliberately 'dumb themselves down'.

Men may say that they like independent women with ambition, who are self-confident, going places, but in practice they prefer women who do not challenge their 'top dog' status in the household, or in an area of expertise they consider their own.

A man dominated by his wife is considered weak – by women too. Both sexes tend to think that a household where the 'woman wears the trousers' is some kind of aberration, inviting pity for the poor hen pecked male, and a fair amount of jocularity. This concept is very rarely heard in the reverse; no surprise or ridicule is expressed when a wife is dominated by her husband. This is as it should be, of course.

Men might try to shift the blame for any unacceptably prejudiced views about women on to historical precedents. It was Aristotle who said: 'Man is by nature superior, and the female inferior: the one rules and the other is ruled.' And St. Paul, no less, wrote in his Epistles to Timothy: 'Women are seen as unsuitable to teach or to have authority over men on the grounds that it was a woman, Eve, who introduced sin into the world.' Sadly, Timothy never wrote back to point out that 'it taketh two to tango'.

To Beauty

Men are genetically programmed to be attracted to beautiful women. They cannot resist. A male praying mantis is attracted to the most alluring female praying mantis – even though she is going to devour him alive while mating.

Beauty is a devastating force, so devastating that it is quite capable of reducing men to gibbering, stumbling, compliant wrecks. Despite all their fantasising, they are actually intimidated by great beauty, and often do not know how to behave when confronted by it. They are more at ease ogling at it on Page 3, or from the safe distance of a cinema seat.

There is a tradition among East Anglian chicken catchers (men who catch chickens for slaughter) that the attractiveness of a woman can be assessed in terms of pints of beer. The system is simple: the more attractive the woman, the fewer pints will be needed to summon up the necessary enthusiasm to commit carnal bliss with her. Some women might be flattered to know that they have been rated 'five-pinters' or even 'four-pinters'. However, after five pints of East Anglian ale most men are incapable of the carnal act anyway.

Real, live, accessible, very beautiful women are in any case rare. Men generally have to settle for something less – though it is probably not half as great a compromise as his opposite number may be making.

To Love

A man experiences love like any other creature: that is, the quickening of the heartbeat, the fresh sense of élan and renewal, the pleasure of intimacy and spontaneous understanding, the inspiration that drives him to put on a clean pair of socks.

He knows he is in love when he finds himself thinking not just about sex every six minutes, but about sex every six minutes with the same woman.

The difference is that men seem to need to be in love rather less than women do before committing themselves to sex. Women would be wise to take any man's profession of love with a pinch of salt. He is likely to be confusing love with lust. If he says 'I love you,' he probably means 'I want sex with you at the earliest possible opportunity.' It's the testosterone again, which may in fact be causing him to make a genuine error, rather than commit to an act of dishonesty. 'But yesterday you swore you'd love me for ever,' complains the jilted girl to her two-timing Lothario. 'I meant it at the time,' he replies.

There are plenty of advertisements for fragrances featuring a beautiful young woman and an (allegedly) stunning young man, both in a state of ecstasy supposedly brought on by the fragrance in question. Men look at the picture of the woman and think, 'She imagines it's for ever.' Then they look at the man and think, 'Rat'.

To Fatherhood

Men have got quite good at fatherhood. Even before their role kicks in, they will attend maternity classes, change the cassette tapes during the birth to provide some suitable background music, and offer encouragement at the head end if they can prevent themselves from passing out. You might like to refer to the survey in which 59% of new mothers declared that their husbands had been supportive. And then move quickly on before anyone can speculate about the remaining 41%.

These days men also do a great deal on the domestic front to help rear the children – like putting an announcement of the birth in one of the national newspapers. Men love children, but few share many women's delight at every primitive offering from the mewling, puking babe. Not until the child is capable of losing to them at football are men really interested in their offspring.

To Feminism

For a while, men faced an even more disturbing threat than the man-eating female: the man-hating female. It was a fairly terrifying experience, a bit like wrestling with an electric fence. There was no place a decent man could put himself without being labelled a 'typical male', the most hurtful of insults.

Fortunately, the spectre of radical feminism has withdrawn from the mainstream. At least men can now join a dinner party without fearing that they might be sitting down with the enemy.

We hesitate to offer an absolute guarantee on this, but it is fairly safe to assume for the purposes of your bluffing that extreme feminism is now regarded as 'old-fashioned'. Even feminist icons such as Professor Camille Paglia have been known to say that men are partly responsible for the civilisation that has given freedom to women – a heresy in previous eras.

Radical feminism contained rather too many home truths for comfort. Men are well aware of their short-comings, and it bemuses them that women generally are so tolerant of them. By the law of opposites, this tolerance can excite male resentment, and is said to be a cause of misogyny.

Some men believe that feminism heralds the end of civilisation as we know it. They blame it for the collapse of family values, the increase in single-parent families, divorce, dysfunctional youth, violent crime and pot noodles. Professor Francis Fukuyama (a name to be handled with care) shows how many of society's ills have grown in parallel to the rise of femi-nism since the 1960s. He calls this effect 'The Great Disruption'. Societies which have maintained tradi-tional male-female roles, like Japan, have not been visited by such moral decline, mainly because a woman dependent on her husband's income is likely to have the stability of the family at heart. Japanese women are not yet in a position to argue.

However, most men's attitudes to feminism remain ambivalent. They can be summed up by the equivocal statement: 'All women become like their mothers. That's their tragedy. No man does. That's his.'

FOIBLES

Wolf-whistling

The male habit of wolf-whistling is based on the tragic misconception that women enjoy such signs of appreciation from strangers, and might even be attracted to the wolf.

A feature of wolf-whistling which is little-noticed (and therefore will do wonders for your image as an authority) is that it is a group activity. A lone male never wolf-whistles. He is usually one of a pack of three or more, often at the safe distance of high-rise scaffolding or moving traffic. The wolf-whistler is, in fact, not so much trying to attract the female, as trying to impress his mates.

Spitting

Football players do it, runners do it, even tennis players do it on the green swards of Wimbledon. Men seem to believe that spit cannot be swallowed. The challenge of hitting an echoing spittoon in Westerns is probably more at fault than anything. But it may be that, like all male animals marking their patch, it is an ancient territorial instinct.

Flies

It is a perpetual concern to men that their flies might be open. They cannot bear the thought of the humiliation if their underpants or, heaven forbid, the family crown jewels were exposed to view. Better the earth should open up and swallow them than that they should leave themselves open to the charge of 'being in a state of undress', 'flying low', or 'not pulling the curtains'.

Italian men surreptitiously touch their balls when they pass a nun in the street, a superstition designed to ward off any threat to their fertility. Most men touch their flies surreptitiously when leaving the loo, to make sure all is safely battened down. Only macho man likes to leave the loo first, and then tug at his zip as though practising for the Olympic Weight Lifting Championships.

Leaving the Seat Up

Life for a man would be a lesser experience if he was not able to unzip his trousers at the edge of the road and pee with glorious abandon into the open countryside. Men were born to urinate standing up, and stand-up urinals best serve this purpose. Sit-down W.C.s are poorly designed for a man, who cannot but help causing some collateral dispersal at this kind of height. It is a mistake to carpet a lavatory.

It is for this reason that a gentleman will always lift the seat. The fact that he is incapable of remembering to put it down again is a permanent irritation to women. 'The seat's up. Dad's home.'

Being able to pee standing up (whether from the stirrups or over the side of a yacht) is the one thing women envy about men. Men tend to keep quiet about their conduit's one imperfection. No matter how much it is shaken, there is always one last drop left in the pipeline.

Sulking

Since men don't, won't or can't talk about emotional matters, they rarely solve an issue by discussing it. Instead they will go into a sulk, cradling their hurt feelings like a small furry animal. They will lapse into a moody silence, broken only by the occasional grunt, or rustle of newspaper. This bad mood may last for days, or even years.

Your male bluffees will be grateful when you point out that they're not to be blamed for sulking. (Your female ones won't, but at least you can rely on them not sulking about it.) Men's heroes and role models have eschewed talking and plumped for direct action. When did anyone ever see John Wayne counselling the Apache, Bruce Willis adopting a therapeutic attitude to Mafia hoods, or Sean Connery conducting a consciousness-raising session with SMERSH?

And men should be given credit for the magnanimous way in which they emerge from their sulk – head hanging, still muttering, ready to forgive their female partner the minute she admits it was all her fault. (Men are at their best when graciously pardoning and forgiving.)

There are two ways to deal with sulking men:

a) ignore them and wait; or
b) attempt to go into a parallel sulk to show them what it is like to live with.

Psychotherapists, you can mention in a casual way, say the first option is the wisest. Then moving from 'casual' to 'world-weary', you can add that they're probably hoping to gain two clients instead of one.

Jokes

Men are better than women at storing the fund of jokes which is in perpetual motion round pubs and parties. It's a good way of ensuring that most precious of social rewards: approval. They are perhaps less inclined to admit that there is one more relevant reason, that men need jokes as reserve stock for conversation when sport fails.

Hobbies

Men are super-active or think they should be. Every moment of the day must be put to good use, so hobbies were invented to occupy their minds during the long periods when they have absolutely nothing to do.

Hobbies annex most of men's spare time and cover a multitude of amazing displacement activities, from building cathedrals out of matchsticks to collecting beermats, old typewriters, hip-flasks, used flashbulbs, calculators which have given up the ghost, and pieces of string too short to use. Pointing this out is an example of that most welcome of creatures, the self-fulfilling bluff. At least one male in your audience will hear the word 'hobby' and automatically launch into an exhaustive account of his own. As detail upon detail tumbles from his tedious lips, everyone else will look upon you with respect that increases by the second.

Sheds

Terminology is always helpful in creating the illusion that you know what you're talking about. Lightly toss in the phrase 'garden shed syndrome', following it up with the explanation that it's what psychologists call a man's innate need to establish his private territory.

Men adore their sheds. Here they can potter around in their old clothes, among tobacco tins filled with miscellaneous screws, and boxes of brackets and bits of twine, humming tunelessly to themselves, breathing in the homely smell of creosote and old flower pots, and perhaps snoozing in a battered old armchair. It is a haven, a comfort zone of their very own.

Their wives should not be jealous – many people pay good money for this kind of therapy.

Tinkering With Cars

Men have to have their toys: laptops, gliders, power drills, power boats, fishing rods, indoor putting kit, trouser press. The most ubiquitous of these is, of course, the car. Women have cars too, but they don't spend their leisure hours tinkering with them – rubbing them sensually with soft cloths, mending them, or stripping them and filling the garage with oily parts.

At the onset of their mid-life crisis, along with the desire to recapture their lost youth, comes a yearning for the sexy, sleek, high-performance car of their dreams – the menoporsche.

But men are touchy about glib references to phallic symbols (even if the car is bright red and called a Probe). They do not see cars as 'penis substitutes' for two reasons:

1. Few men can afford a Lexus or a Ferrari.
2. There is no substitute for a penis.

PRACTICALITIES

Men at Work

Men are apt to define themselves by their work – a rather tragic state of affairs given the extraordinary amount of dull labour that is required to keep the world turning. When a man talks to another man, he is dying to know first and foremost what the other one does, so that he can place him. Otherwise he is at a bit of a loss.

But you must remember, as you engage a man in

conversation, that it is simply not allowed to ask him directly, 'what do you do ?' Certainly men themselves never operate like this. Instead, they tease the information from each other by talking about everything else – golf, cars, football, insurance – constantly looking for clues. When they have discovered the other one's profession, they can relax; then go through the conversation all over again and actually listen to what is being said.

At work, men have to treat other men carefully. They have to establish an understanding that suggests 'I'm not a threat to you, so let's work together and get the job done'. Otherwise there is hostility, and the next thing is they are outside with their antlers locked.

Men's obsession with work means that they are particularly prone to crisis on being made redundant: it is not just their job that has gone, but their vision of themselves as individuals.

In these days of sexual equality in the workplace it is dangerous to suggest that men are better than women in any particular field – although quite permissible to trumpet the reverse. It doesn't really matter, however, as men are powerful self-deceivers and great believers in what other men say. So, even though all men may know they are inferior to women, as long as other men say they are superior, that will be enough to restore their self-confidence.

Another area in which men appear to have the edge, and both male and female employers seem to agree, is risk-taking. Women bosses, for instance, often prefer male assistants because they will make decisions off their own bat and take the initiative to get things done. Risk of disapproval is involved. Successful risk-taking often makes the difference in advancing a business. Of course, there is also a downside: catastrophe.

Sadly, for most men work usually takes precedence over the family. Even if it's not in their original game plan, it just seems to happen, sidling up to them and then hijacking them. They pretend to be happy to leave the home early and return late, but this is just another example of men's amazing ability to deceive themselves. They may creep into a pub and assert to their mates that they'd rather be sharing a pint than reading bedtime stories to their children, but only a mate on a similar self-deceiving binge would believe them. If you're confident that your discussion is in a phase light-hearted enough to cope with this, you can mention the tragic truth that many men often only start to see their children on access weekends after the divorce.

Working With Women

Men are coming to terms with having women as colleagues at work and even accepting them as seniors.

This does not come easily. Men are used to ruling the roost in the workplace: they have been doing so for thousands of years. It accounts for many of the traditional male attitudes which irk their female associates, principally:

- allowing the sight of a short skirt to affect their decisions
- leaving all the lights blazing
- expecting their own views to hold sway.

Men realise that there are many aspects of business which women do better than them. But they make these concessions from a position of strength. Statistics show that 89% of managers are men, so women have still not broken through the 'glass ceiling' sufficiently to challenge men at the top. But then men do not incubate human beings nor, for the most part, run homes or rear families. A suitably cynical note to strike here is that this arrangement is a great relief: otherwise what chance would they have?

It is said that men are better suited to the cut and thrust of the workplace. Apart from having more muscle, they have been trained on the school sports field to be team players, and to look up to the captain.

Because the area in the brain which produces sympathy is less active in men, they are better able to cope with confrontation, to hire and fire. But though this gave them a head start, the working world has changed to one in which traditional female virtues of communication and mutually beneficial compromise are increasingly valued. Men are having to adapt. (This does not mean they are willing to learn how to put new paper in the photocopier. Such roles are assigned to women – along with collecting their dry cleaning, selecting birthday cards for their wives, and ignoring telephone conversations beginning 'I told you not to ring me here'.)

There is also a fair amount of ogling, bottom-patting and lewd comment, considered by men to be part of their civil liberties, until defined as sexual harassment. A key aspect of successful bluffing is never to get too serious, so should this topic arise we recommend a quick escape via a comment to the effect that men find it difficult to differentiate between friendly banter which acknowledges gender-differences and a bit of harmless flirting on the one hand, and what is deemed offensive behaviour on the other. As in all things, they can be guaranteed to overstep the mark on occasions, if not regularly.

Men feel they have made great strides in owning that new rules apply. It cannot be helped if some of them harbour resentment that certain successful women in work and business exploit their femininity to ruthless effect. It does, however, mean that men, too, can now be accused of sleeping their way to the top.

Domesticity

It is hard for a man to substitute a woman for the domestic virtues of bachelor life, the manly pleasures of:
- leaving the bed unmade
- belching ad lib
- using every pot in the kitchen.

Your bluffees may scoff when you assert that men are no less capable of looking after the home than women. But that scoff is an investment well worth your making. Let their derision abate, and point them to the evidence. It is widely accepted, for instance, that landlords prefer to have single men as tenants, because they keep the place looking reasonably tidy, even a little unoccupied. Also, single men often resent sharing a house with single women, who leave their undies soaking in the washbasin, use more loo paper, and treat the house as a changing-room. Your words will have all the more effect for having proved such an unlikely proposition. This is the bluffing equivalent of walking on water, and will establish you as an expert no-one dares challenge

You must also, however, have comments ready to keep the women you're addressing on board. Surveys, for instance, have shown that, in couples where both partners are working, women still do six hours more housework per week. This may mean that only six hours of housework are being done in all. Such statistics reflect traditional divisions of labour by gender. But they may also relate to the fact that domestic chores tend to be done by the person with the greater sensitivity to dirty loos, grimy baths, sticky lino and overflowing laundry-baskets – and this is usually a woman. Men have the advantage of being thick-skinned; they approach the state of the house rather like the Three Wise Monkeys – see no evil, feel no evil, smell no evil.

Any woman prepared to see just how filthy a man would allow his home to be before he did anything about it, would have to wait a long time. Quentin Crisp once remarked that the nice thing about doing no housework is that after three years there doesn't seem to be any observable increase in the dust. This was one of the rare occasions when he spoke for almost all men.

But men have an increasingly uneasy attitude to housework. They don't mind leaving it undone, but they feel decidedly guilty if their female partner does it all. New Man likes to do his share. This usually means 'helping with' the washing up, the hoovering, and taking the smaller rubbish bin to the bigger one outside. The unspoken message is clear. It's still all the duty of the woman, but the male lends an occasional hand.

Shopping

You can safely assert that the majority of men dislike shopping. It not only means spending money, but making snap decisions. They like armchair shopping first, studying advertisements, comparing prices before going out to buy a car, a house, farmland, a factory, a company or an international corporation. The purchase of a lettuce, cat food or air freshener does not excite them.

A man will be happy for a while in a hardware shop if he badly needs a hammer or 200 yards of plastic tubing. But shopping, in general, seems to him to be a waste of time. A mega waste of time as far as he is concerned, is window shopping. This he does not understand at all. The joy of staring at goods for sale which cannot be bought because the shop is closed is quite beyond his comprehension.

Dress Sense

Young men might choose to buy collarless shirts, crocodile shoes and Dennis-the-Menace socks, but once into their middle age, men rarely buy any clothes at all. There is a tasty little marketing secret with which you can amuse people should talk turn to this subject: advertisements for male underwear are placed in locations where women will see them, not because this turns women on (which is what men like to think), but simply because it is the women who buy them. It is a tradition that starts with their mothers, is taken up by their girlfriends and ends with their wives.

Alternatively, you might demonstrate the 'men are disinterested in clothes' thesis by asking one of your male bluffees when he last bought himself a pair of underpants. He is quite likely to avoid the question. Wait for him to refer to the fabulous set of silky underclothes he bought for his girlfriend or wife – skimpy, lacy, revealing, with suspenders. Then reply: "Just what she always wanted." But take care to inject the comment with sufficient humour. Causing members of the audience to walk away never reflects well on a bluffer.

Most men will vacuum the entire house or start concreting the drive rather than go to a clothes shop. They will adopt a set of tatty clothes in which they feel most comfortable for all the hours outside work – a favourite woolly jumper, frayed jeans or kneed cords and a T-shirt advertising some nostalgic memory of misspent youth. Making them part with them is like separating a baby from its comforter.

Similarly, many men appear welded, as well as wedded, to their socks – despite clear evidence that wandering round the bedroom dressed only in stretch nylon (sizes 8 to 11) makes them look about as sexy as suet pudding. This is not some form of perversion, it's linear thinking. Socks are the last item of clothing to be removed. They remain on the top of the heap of clothes overnight, and so are the first to be put on in the morning. And men are nothing if not creatures of habit.

Many men are frightened of looking sexy, feeling that this is the province of women, and that there is something essentially female about being concerned with one's looks at all. What does it matter to a man if the elastic has gone in his Y fronts? What's wrong with underpants so old that they have taken on the colour of storm cloud and the texture of wire wool? Minimalist designs and silky fabrics are for lingerie freaks, not for real men. Offer the thought that were men to wear something soft next to their skin, the next you know they'd be behaving like women: waxing their legs, changing their minds, and gossiping.

Shaving

Men shave because it's a macho occupation. They love the terrifying scrape of cold steel across the face, the delicate work round the lips, the surgical precision needed at the entrances to the nostrils, the scars so bravely borne when things go wrong. It's the nearest they get to the duelling clubs of Old Heidelberg. Besides which, shaving is the one skill men possess that nobody has taught them.

Shaving is a ritual that shapes the day. Men's

facial hair grows at the rate of about 12 inches a year, and it takes on average about two and a half days each year to keep it under control. So it gives a man ample opportunity to admire himself regularly in the mirror without arousing the least suspicion that he is vain.

Young men seem unsure at present whether to shave or not – designer stubble attracts young women but alienates their mothers. Men who grow beards are thought by many to be hiding a sense of inferiority, which they frequently are. But before the invention of breakfast cereals, which are known to have a magnetic attraction to beards, men made full cosmetic use of facial hair, sporting extravagant sideboards, handlebar moustaches, pencil moustaches, goatees and beards like lion's manes. Untrimmed beards could reach enormous proportions – the longest recorded was over 17 feet. Today, if men don't shave, their wives may complain of the bristles. They may also compare them to a lavatory brush, and tell them to stand upside down next to the loo to make themselves useful.

Sport

It is generally believed that men play sports for their health. This is only partly true. Most take exercise as a kind of balancing act. They heave and sweat around the rugby pitch in order to make space for the quantity of beer they will later consume.

Sport serves two useful functions for men, apart from keeping fit:

1. It tires them out.

2. It gives them something to talk about. Most young men develop an interest in sport because it is a way of communicating with their fathers.

53

Three out of four men take part in some form of sport every week, while just over half of women feel the need. Women play sports to lose weight and participate; men play sports to win. Even when they are pounding the footpaths in a late-night jog they are secretly pounding the table at a conference, flooring their rivals with their sharpened acumen.

Sport also provides the best excuse for unbridled behaviour, such as spitting, shouting, swearing, scratching the testicles, and flattening others – and all that while watching television.

TOUCHY SUBJECTS

Giving up Seats

There was a time when men would open doors for women, and unhesitatingly offer their seat on public transport. During the great years of strident feminism such behaviour might have been rewarded with a stern lecture. Men learnt to get on a bus or a train without looking sideways, and instantly bury their heads in a newspaper.

Yet many men still feel an atavistic urge to give way to women. They are not actually reading those papers, but staring blankly at the print while they assess whether the woman standing over them is pregnant or decrepit enough to justify rising. These are the men who have all made critical mistakes in the past – the grey-haired female who did not appreciate being labelled as old and frail; the woman with a weight problem who did not realise it was quite that bad. Some men in the throes of this dilemma will never come to anyone's notice – they don't dare sit down at all.

Seeking Advice

Men like to sort out their own problems. Only if they cannot do so will they reluctantly seek the advice and help of others. It puts them in an awkward position: it makes them look weak and vulnerable.

Neither men nor women, but particularly women, should volunteer advice to a man, especially about a manly task. A delightful trick to play when discussing this topic is to adopt a sombre demeanour, then offer your listeners the following tip: if any of them – and God forbid they should – ever find themselves in the position of having to give a man advice (in order, for instance, to prevent a disaster), they must – *must* – disguise it as support, and preferably try to make it look as if it was his idea in the first place.

Height

The ideal man projected by films, advertising and classical myths is athletic and tall – qualities that by extension are also associated with virtues such as courage, loyalty, honesty, and an immediate advantage in the basketball team. Height seems to express authority. In the 20th century, 80% of U.S. presidential elections were won by the taller candidate.

Short men are very conscious of their standing. It is often suggested that they compensate by exaggerated behaviour that gets them noticed, by becoming tyrannical, witty or enormously rich. But nothing compensates for the uncomfortable fact that they have to look up to the other men and, worse still, look up to many women. Women offer little consolation: most say that they would prefer a man taller than themselves as a partner. In only one marriage in 720 is the woman taller than the man, and veteran film star Mickey Rooney (5 ft 1 ins), married eight times, accounts for more than his fair share of them.

Short men will rarely admit that they are short, or want to talk about it. If the conversation is unavoidable, you might like to list some famous men who are, or were, vertically challenged: Wayne Sleep is 5 ft 2 ins (1.57 m); Humphrey Bogart was 5 ft 4 ins (1.62 m). Tom Cruise is 5 ft 5½ ins (1.66 m), Al Pacino is 5 ft 6 ins (1.67 m), as was Frank Sinatra; John Lennon was 5 ft 7 ins (1.70 m) and so is Sylvester Stallone and Mick Jagger; though these statistics should be given maximum headroom since no celebrity is likely to submit to being measured against a doorjamb.

Being Single

Being a bachelor has little of the stigma attached to being 'an old maid'. Once over a certain age, a single male becomes eligible for the epithet 'confirmed bachelor', a term which is now open to interpretation of the nudge-nudge, wink-wink kind. This is about the one aspect of single men's lives that does not turn married men green with envy. That, and their shorter life expectancy (by some 5 years) than married ones.

Single men are highly sensitive to the fact that the rest of the world is couple-oriented. Their friends are constantly trying to marry them off, as if trying to ensure that everyone is infected with the same virus – a sort of societal inoculation against envy of the single state.

That Time of the Month

Men cannot bear talking about menstruation. They don't even like to think about it. In Bali, menstruating women are exiled to huts outside the village compound because they are held to be vulnerable to evil spirits. To many men that seems just about right: menstruation represents the direct opposite to everything a woman is supposed to be.

The very idea of it makes men blush. There is only one thing worse: when men try to talk about it frankly and honestly. Then women blush.

Castration

This is one to avoid. Most men will deny that they have a castration complex, which may simply encourage you to feel that Sigmund Freud was probably right to suggest that they did.

Not that this ground is entirely barren from a bluffer's point of view. Raise the subject of Lorena Bobbit, who in 1993 severed her husband's penis with a kitchen knife. Then remind everyone that she was acquitted, and enjoy watching all the men squirm. This will do very little for your status as an expert, but at least it will give you a laugh. Why should your bluffees have all the fun?

Circumcision

Sanitary considerations seem to be at the root of male circumcision. It has been practised among the ancient Egyptians, the Incas of Peru, all Muslims, all Jews, many African tribes and the Australian aborigines. What they all have in common is the desert, and everyone knows how pernicious sand is.

These days men do not so frequently come with this option. In the U.K. fewer than 10% of boys are now circumcised. But they remain concerned about which model women prefer – Roundheads or Cavaliers.

Many women seem uneasy about the idea of such mutilation, though they may express a preference for its aesthetic effects. It is principally circumcised men who are used in nude photographs. Women also attest that the Roundhead is a better stayer because it has been exposed to years of inside-trouser friction. Mention that around a dinner table and you will soon divine who is which.

Shape

Men are conscious of their bodies. They have seen women swoon over the rippling biceps and washboard stomachs of the superstars. But it is a hard task for most men to achieve this kind of physique without immense effort, and they soon suspect that they do not need to bother.

One in three men believe that they are overweight and are worried about the shape of their stomach. Yet after the age of 40, many men secretly accept that they will never see their feet again. 'Take me as I am,' they declare, and many woman do.

Snoring

This is a hardy perennial for those bluffing about men, due to its near-perfect combination of ubiquity and comic value. Be prepared for men to go on the defensive; most of them spend their lives being criticised for snoring. Keep them on your side by revealing that women snore as well. It's just that women are the lighter sleepers, so wake up more often to the vibrating sounds in their partner's soft palate and so-called 'posterior faucal pillars'.

Snoring occurs when lying face up, so various precautions can be taken. A sheet of sandpaper can be sewn into the back of the pyjama top, for example, or a hairbrush can be placed in the trousers. Whistling in the snorer's ear often changes the sleep pattern and stops the snoring. Other than that, it's best if he sleeps in another room.

Hypochondria

It is widely held that women can bear more pain than men – that men could not tolerate the excruciating pain of childbirth. This proposition will be triumphantly shot down by men using the argument that it can never be put to the test.

Meanwhile, men make a great play of putting up with ailments. They will happily go to work with a thick cold, sneeze and cough all day, infect everyone else in the effort to convince them that they are martyrs to their work, then take the next two weeks off.

Lurking behind their bravado, however, is a strange contradiction. When men are ill, it is never with anything trivial. A sore throat could be laryngitis, a touch of indigestion may be the onset of renal failure, tiredness is exhaustion, pins and needles may presage cardiac arrest, a spot could well be skin cancer. They convince themselves they may be going to die.

This fear will not lead them to the doctor. They don't want to hear they are going to die. Neither do they want to be told that they have nothing more than a minor indisposition. They would rather die.

In fact, not going to the doctor means that men run

the risk of contracting long-term illnesses that could have been diagnosed earlier. It may also account to some extent for the fact that men have a shorter average life expectancy than women, by five years – 74 as opposed to 79. But men, being silent martyrs to their ailments, are most intolerant of women who complain legitimately of theirs. 'Yes, I had that last week,' they will assert, and this sentence continues in a think-bubble over their head, 'and I didn't make that kind of fuss.' Women's illnesses are inconvenient, exaggerated and, worst of all, could upstage their own.

Grey Hair

It is said that men with grey hair, or greying temples, look more distinguished, more attractive and more intelligent than those without. This is of course a myth put out by clever wives and girlfriends.

The astute grey-haired man will douse his scalp liberally with a product which turns his hair to a shade of mid-mouse, knowing that it takes years off his age. It may – possibly – be worth reminding people that they should never draw attention to discernable tints in a man's hair. But on no account should you say that it will lead to 'hairy moments'. Nothing diminishes a bluffer's standing more than a feeble joke.

No Hair

Men need some comfort about hair loss. It is best if they go bald when they are about 23, when they still believe they have other things going for them. At 45 they need consolation; denial is something they can do for themselves.

The Japanese have always associated baldness with high levels of sexual activity. In fact, they are thinking of excessive sexual activity and reprehensible dissipation, which is deemed both damaging and ridiculous, but you do not have to mention this. Nor the fact that in some parts of the Far East, baldness is so rare that when people come across it, they just fall about laughing.

Men think that hair – real or false – is a sine qua non of sex appeal, and no amount of reasoning will tell them otherwise. Women consistently say that baldness doesn't matter; that bald men are attractive; that, after all, they adore babies and most of them are bald. But if cornered by a man insisting that truly, honestly, he really does not mind a pristine pate – you should offer reassurance by quoting some scientific evidence for the idea that bald men are sexier. It has been shown that testosterone directly affects hair growth by starving hair roots in the scalp in order to apply itself elsewhere.

A new treatment for baldness which encourages hair growth contains an agent prohibiting the production of dihydrotestosterone. The trouble is that this results in a loss of sex drive, which is somewhat counterproductive.

Should you by any chance find yourself conversing on this topic with a follicly-challenged man who has, for whatever reason, lost your sympathy, you could amuse yourself by telling him that there is one guaranteed method of restoring up to 40% of hair loss. Wait for his eager cry of 'Oh really, what's that?' Then inform him that it's castration.

But it's a bit of an extreme measure.

THINGS MEN SHOULD TELL OTHER MEN ABOUT WOMEN

It's easier to share your life with a dog than a woman because:

Dogs like it if you leave a lot of things on the floor.

The later you are, the more delighted dogs are to see you.

A dog's disposition stays the same all month long.

If a dog leaves, it won't take half your stuff.

A dog won't wake you up at night to ask, 'If I died, would you get another dog?'

* * * *

A woman always has the last word in any argument. Anything a man says after that is the beginning of a new argument.

Men play at love to get sex. Women play at sex to get love.

A woman marries a man expecting him to change, but he doesn't. A man marries a woman expecting that she won't change, but she does.

* * * *

Women are like computers because:

Only the Creator understands their internal logic.

Even your smallest mistakes are stored in long-term memory for later retrieval.

The Error message is about as informative as 'If you don't know what's wrong, I'm certainly not going to tell you.'

GLOSSARY

Andropause – The male menopause. The jury is still out on whether this is a valid concept; some call it 'getting old'.

Bachelor – Man who gets tangled up with a number of women in order to avoid getting tied up with one.

Condom – Contraceptive device which doubles as a brake.

Family crown jewels – Reproductive organs; also referred to as equipment, wedding tackle, meat and two veg, the dangly bits, and the full Monty.

Friend – Someone to whom a man can admit sexual disaster, having already failed to buy his round.

Fwaw! – An expression of appreciation of female sexual desirability by one who has already decided that he has no hope of fulfilling it.

Gentleman – One who takes the weight on his knees and elbows.

Husband – A man who has given himself the opportunity of committing another sin, adultery.

Impotence – Spending all night trying to do once what you once spent all night doing.

Man's man – One who exemplifies what men want to find in men.

Mate – Not the woman a man is sleeping with, but the chap who shares a six-pack with him when his team has won the Cup.

Men – Boys who have finished growing.

Misogynist – Hater of women. No known inverse. An ancient Greek word; Plato thought women should be classed with children and slaves.

Nymphomaniac – A woman who appreciates sex in almost the same quantity and breadth as men.

Penis – The male organ, also known as Bishop, chopper, cock, dick, dong, John Thomas, knob, one-eyed trouser snake, pecker, percy, plonker, pork sword, prick, prong, skyscraper, tail, tassel, todger, tool, wick, widger, willy, winkie, whirley-wha (Scots).

Polygamy – One man, many wives; a male fantasy, until he works out the cost.

Rat – A rival, a.k.a. cad, bounder, knave, rotter, two-timing bastard.

Testicles – Sperm manufacturing units; a.k.a. balls, bollocks, cojones, gonads, goolies, pocket billiards, testes, knackers and nuts.

Testosterone – The male hormone which gives men their virile qualities, their sex drive, and their smell.

Wanker – A man who masturbates; hence, effectively, any man.

Wet dream – Nocturnal emissions. The male sex drive's way of saying who is boss.

Wife – A woman who sticks with her husband through all the troubles he wouldn't have had if he hadn't married her.

Womaniser – One who has the success with women that all men envy, a.k.a. rake, philanderer, wolf, stud, lucky swine.

W.H.T. – Wandering hand trouble, a feature of the inept womaniser, and the dirty old man.

WOMEN

CONTENTS

THE KEY TO UNDERSTANDING WOMEN

There isn't one.

Since the beginning of time, women have induced ecstasy, provoked murder, caused wars, and hung their pantyhose on the shower rail – all the while proclaiming ignorance of what the fuss is about.

Men, who generally claim to know everything worth knowing, are happy to admit that they cannot understand women. As Thackeray put it: 'When I say that I know women, I mean I know that I don't know them. Every single woman I ever knew is a puzzle to me, as, I have no doubt, she is to herself.'

The little known fact of the matter is that both sexes rather like to perpetuate this belief. Women enjoy the feeling of being all-knowing but unknowable: it gives them a rare edge. Men like to absolve themselves from the need to work it out – without a sense of personal failure. If *no* man can understand women, it's not his fault if he doesn't.

So an aspiring expert has plenty of leeway for error. Which is just as well, because even when you have read this guide you may feel that, although you know a lot more, you are still none the wiser. However, you may be heartened to know immediately that there are a great many things about women that even women don't understand.

When discussing women, therefore, it is useful to assume that no-one has the faintest idea what they are talking about, and the person who wins the argument on the subject can only be a bluffer.

ESSENTIAL DIFFERENCES

'Men and women are now held to be equal, but they are not the same.' This is a remark which will pay eternal dividends on your investment in memorising it. You'll be able to work it into just about any discussion of the sexes, safe in the knowledge that no-one will disagree, be they die-hard males who defiantly see women as flawed versions of themselves, or women in boiler suits who see men as superfluous.

While men believe themselves to be ordinary, common or garden members of the human race (well, never that ordinary, of course) women know they are different, something apart. They have a perspective on the world that is uniquely their own.

Body Design

Whatever the standpoint, no-one can dispute that men and women are built to totally different specifications:

a) Women are rounder, softer to the touch and smell a lot better.

b) Women's most essential equipment is kept tidily within the engine housing. Men have an exterior telescopic urinary device that seems to have a mind of its own.

c) Women's bodies naturally contain more fat – 25% of their body weight, compared with 12½% in men's. This has advantages as insurance against cold and as an aid to buoyancy.

d) Unlike men, women have useful breasts that can produce milk when called upon and store fat for times of famine. In fact, only one third of the breast is devoted to the function of lactation, the rest is food-storage. As it happens, big breasts do not necessarily mean successful breast-feeding because they can get clogged with fat glands which obstructs milk-production. It is a well-known maxim of the farmyard that you shouldn't buy a fat cow.

e) Women are equipped with a magical component that transforms men's impetuous spermatozoa into human beings.

The XX Factor

Every human has a string of 23 pairs of chromosomes (the genetic markers that carry hereditary features such as blue eyes, knock knees and preferred choice of cocktail). Until the seventh week after conception, the foetus is gender-dormant but at this point, if the child is to be male, the solitary 'Y' in its XY pair of sex chromosomes kicks in – and the production of another little lord and master is set in motion. If the child is to be a female, its XX sex chromosome ensures that the foetus continues blithely on its female path.

The female, therefore, can be seen as what, in computer technology, is termed the 'default' programme – that is, the one the machine is coded to use unless instructed otherwise. You may wish to use this analogy when bluffing to Creationist Christians: clearly Eve was not made from Adam's rib, Adam is simply a chip off the eternal Eve.

A key technique which you must master if you want to indulge in socially-adept bluffing is that of adapting your material to the situation at hand. Should you wish to sound a note sympathetic to males, argue that the creative input of the male Y chromosome represents something positive and clever in itself. If, however, the need is for the opposite view, say that as maleness is only accounted for by 1/46th of a person's heredity, it's very small beer. Or in Zsa-Zsa Gabor's words: 'Macho doesn't mean mucho.'

The XX factor has a number of advantages over the XY:

- Women are less prone to colour blindness.

- Women have a more acute sense of hearing, taste, smell and touch.

- Women's eyes adjust faster, so they can see better in the dark, useful for slamming the alarm clock button before dawn.

The XX chromosome also carries a socialising gene, the 'sugar and spice and all things nice' of the nursery rhyme. The male lacks this ready-made factor. He has to learn to be nice.

Scientists are likely to claim that it is hard enough identifying the genes that cause major illnesses, let alone something as vague and fancy as socialising genes. But bluffers should never allow circumspection to get in the way of a good idea.

Blame Oestrogen

It is the sex hormone oestrogen that effectively makes a woman a woman. Produced chiefly in her ovaries, oestrogen brings about a woman's metamorphosis at puberty from beanbag to egg-timer, activates her womb and controls her moon-like cycle. It is the decline in oestrogen production in late middle age that sets off the menopause and makes women vulnerable to brittle bones. The male equivalent is testosterone, produced by the testes (balls to most of us).

Because oestrogen governs the way their bodies are formed, including their brains, hormones really do affect women's behaviour. Hence a woman's entitlement to blame them for:

- being assailed by lurid fantasies about the window cleaner
- purchasing tins of floor polish when the whole house is carpeted wall to wall
- snapping at her husband for mislaying her keys
- Bobbitting her partner for playing away while he is under the influence of testosterone.

Oestrogen is metabolised by the liver which might explain why women have a lower alcohol tolerance than men, especially when at their most fertile – their bodies are too busy making them fecund to process the booze. This may also be nature's crafty way of ensuring that a woman is at her most uninhibited at the very best time to conceive.

The Brain

Women's brains are also constructed differently. Men's brains are on average bigger by about five ounces – the weight of a small hamburger, without the bun.

There is a widespread awareness that the sexes' brains differ physically. Widespread, but unclear. Few people know the details. And as any seasoned bluffer will tell you, details about something people have already heard of are the keys that unlock the door of Implied Expertise. Provide facts about a theory that no-one is aware of and you'll appear clever but irrelevant. But provide facts that fill in the gaps in their existing knowledge, and you'll excite their curiosity, tickle the underbelly of their intellect. The details in question here are: women's brains contain a higher concentration of cells in the cortices associated with listening and language ability, have a bigger passageway connecting the left and right hemispheres of the brain, and more movement of signals between the two hemispheres. Having wowed your listeners with this, you can go on to say that this may explain why, as some observers claim, men have a linear way of thinking, while women's thought patterns follow a more circular configuration – which could be another way of saying that men think only of one thing, while women just go on and on.

It also means that women:

- learn to talk earlier than men (there are signs that they start practising with their lips while still in the womb)

- display greater manual dexterity (female fingers are better at finicky jobs like computer assembly, sutures and applying nail-varnish)

- are less prone to dyslexia and stuttering

- have more acute verbal skills ('Wha'dda ya mean where's your dinner? Your dinner is in the dog.')

- pay more attention to detail. If a group of boys and girls are asked to draw a house, the boys will almost always draw the framework first, then add a chimney, whereas girls concentrate on the doors and windows (with curtains).

- chart a route by focusing on landmarks, rather than map or compass ('There was a bent lamppost on the corner'). Many men believe that women navigate conversations the same way.

Virtually any conversation in mixed company will provide at least one or two examples of such differences for you to pluck out and use in your bluffing.

Once an example has been provided, you can go on to explain how these tendencies have been reinforced culturally over the aeons. In the past, when men went off in droves armed with weapons in search of bison or any spare women they fancied, talk was superfluous. They could survive with grunts and hand signals. Meanwhile, the women were stuck in the cave with the babies – an environment which called for nurture, empathy and good communications:

> 'I've been at him for moons to fix that rock in the roof, but he's done nothing.'
> 'These berries are definitely the best for tenderising aardvark.'
> 'Personally, I wouldn't touch him with a spear pole.'
> 'That's the last time I'm telling you – don't draw on the walls.'

GUILES AND GUISES

Whereas men go through various distinct phases in growing up (to use the term loosely) but end up as basically the same model, women encompass a bewildering variety of different types. They have a battery of disguises at their disposal, and select the ones that best suit them to achieve their own ends.

To complicate matters further, many of the guises overlap, and most women are capable of switching between even wildly incompatible ones to match the occasion. And since, to a woman, an occasion may be as brief as an argument-clinching sentence or a passing greeting, she can often seem to epitomise the full range simultaneously.

The system being far from foolproof, we advise that you refrain from promising your audience a comprehensive analysis, and stick instead to mentioning a few general traits:

Poor Little Me

Soft-spoken, prettily self-deprecating, and with a whim of iron, Poor Little Me has discovered early on that the helpless female usually gets everything done for her by indulgent parents and older siblings.

Seeing no reason to change a winning formula as she grows up, she makes great play of her physical feebleness, mechanical and intellectual incompetence and general dependence, and thus almost always gets her own way with minimum amount of trouble to herself.

In painting a picture of this behaviour you will strike chords that resonate in virtually every one of your listeners. Men will recognise the technique as it is often a great success with them – their egos are easily flattered – while women are usually irritated or even infuriated by it. Knowing that women can always cope, they despise Poor Little Me's pretence that she can't; they feel she is letting the side down by trading on the erroneous stereotype of the helpless female, and resent her easy entrapment of gullible would-be knights-errant. Above all, of course, they are jealous of her rate of success.

The downside is that Poor Little Me can become as clingy as she intended to be. Few men see through her because she dazzles them. Even other women find her hard to unmask. Observe people's knowing smiles as you remind them how impossible it is to win an argument with someone who says sweetly and simperingly: 'I'm sure you're right, it's just that I have no memory/am so stupid about money/don't understand anything mechanical,' and then goes serenely on to do exactly what she wanted to and they swore they wouldn't countenance.

Bimbo

The oddest thing about Bimbos is that they really don't seem to mind the label. This could mean that they are as air-headed as the image they project, or it could mean they have everything much better sussed than anyone gives them credit for. After all, it must be quite relaxing to sail through life turning heads, eager to be attentive to a series of egotistical males, and ready to party at the drop of a wallet.

On the surface, Bimbos have much in common with 'Poor Little Me's, but they lack the manipulativeness – all they want is a good time. Most women, and about a quarter of men, deride them, but fairly indulgently: the general view tends to be that they really can't help it. Besides, the phenomenon is temporary. Bimbos mysteriously vanish in their mid-twenties, becoming trophy wives if they're lucky, or doormats if they aren't.

Should you encounter a man who needs to divest himself of the attentions of a bimbo, remind him of one simple truth: bimbos are not subtle, and therefore their game is easily routed. Just stop paying.

Doormat

The Doormat subsumes all her own interests to the needs and demands of her family. Her husband, well aware that he should be contributing more to the housekeeping/parenting role than he does, but unwilling to forego the luxury of dinner on the table and his clothes picked up after him, tends to placate rather than help. Other women may talk bracingly to the Doormat about Open University courses, but will generally give up under a barrage of counter-arguments.

It is in nobody's interests for Doormats to change their ways. They are too useful as reliable cooks/bottlewashers, emergency baby-sitters, errand runners and servicemen-letter-inners. Counsel your bluffees that the best way to deal with Doormats is to do what what most people do, and use them shamelessly.

Earth Mother

The carer par excellence, she is programmed to understand and provide for everything anybody might need or want: she would embrace the whole human race if she could.

In childhood, Earth Mothers patiently mind younger siblings; at university they indulgently make coffee and toast at 3 a.m. for drunken fellow students searching for the meaning of life; in adulthood they nurture their own brood, any they may have inherited, those of their friends and neighbours, plus multifarious godchildren; at work they are the ones who answer plaintive phones on unattended desks.

They are admirable. But Earth Mothers unfortunately know what's good for everyone. As they cluck around their wholefood kitchen, breastfeeding the four year old, they dispense endless homilies on how to sort out your own inadequate life. Ultimately they miss out, because people learn to avoid any area of conversation which might engender their voluminous advice.

Ballbreaker

Ballbreakers come in two distinct varieties: the ardent feminist to whom men are always, implacably, the enemy; and the intimidating career woman who manages to be feminine, sexy, and efficient at juggling work, family and leisure. Both kinds are just as alarming to women as they are to men.

Accordingly people will respect you if in your capacity as an 'authority' on women you can offer a tip or two on how to deal with ballbreakers. Tell them they can disarm a feminist by agreeing earnestly with her on all points, and then going away and carrying on in their own sweet way. Say it is even possible to undermine a super-achiever by quoting some of the statistics and opinions that have arisen in the course of the backlash against the concept of having (or doing) it all. "But," you should confide in a jaded tone of voice, "if a ballbreaker is really entrenched in her role, you will almost certainly fail. Better to express unqualified admiration for her, and admit the shortcomings that make you personally unable to compete".

Normal

This guise is the most cunning of them all. Women are never normal. Each and every one of them knows that she is utterly extraordinary and enigmatic.

SEX

Women need to feel a degree of sexual intimacy before sex becomes desirable. They need a sense of security and comfort, free from distraction, where they can relax and enjoy the totality of a deeply sensual experience – and probably black-out conditions to shield them from reality.

A chat-provoking survey to keep up your sleeve is the one in which nearly a third of women said they could 'take or leave sex' and 80% said they get more pleasure from food. Paradoxically, almost the same percentage believed that they derived as much pleasure from sex as men. Point out that women bring to sex a rather different mind-set: they are more interested in how they are treated than in performance ratings. For women, intimacy sometimes results in sex; for men, sex sometimes results in intimacy.

But we must warn you against the mistake of extrapolating from this that women do not have a corresponding sex drive. (The Careless Extrapolation: a poisonous beast, is one of the bluffer's deadliest enemies.) Women do have a strong sex drive – especially when the oestrogen levels are right. Yet, whereas a man is bundled along by his testosterone-inflated sex drive, and may become physically uncomfortable if he goes more than a week without ejaculating, a woman can go for years without sex, applying a form of self-control of which most men are incapable. In Britain the average woman has 3.4 sexual partners over a lifetime – although nobody will admit to being the one who was only point four.

Virginity

This once-cherished notion has been largely suspended through lack of volunteers. Statistically it was on a hiding to nothing. If all men want to experiment before marrying a virgin, there is inevitably going to be a shortfall.

Men, if they give it a thought, believe that the hymen is a redoubtable membrane with the consistency of bubblegum. They may be confounded or relieved to discover that, because of energetic sports and use of tampons, many women barely have one to speak of. Women's experience of the 'first time' varies, and is less related to the resistance of the hymen than to the skill of their partners. Women divide into those who hardly noticed its breach, and those who would rather draw a veil over the whole event.

There is a tale of a young couple emerging from a quickie in the dark. The somewhat chastened man remarked that had he known the girl was a virgin, he would have gone about the matter more slowly. The girl retorted that had she understood his hurry, she would have removed her tights first.

Seduction

Traditionally, men make the first move. Or so they like to believe.

In fact, it is nearly always women who seduce men. They send out little signals with their eyes, they touch an arm, they remove an imaginary hair from a man's sleeve. Then comes a bit of feminine sleight of hand: they make a tactical retreat. It is not long before the average male comes charging down the hill with the whiff of the chase in his nostrils.

When men say they find a certain woman attractive, they often mean they think she is available, or at least that she is putting out availability signals (otherwise known as flirting). Men like to think they know how to read these signals, but unfortunately are probably not as good at doing so as other women – such as their wives.

A woman knows that there is no better way to cultivate a man's interest than to make him yearn for her – the time-honoured convention of 'playing hard to get'. This is done by adhering to some tried and tested rules, such as:

- delay answering his telephone messages
- never be free on the first date he suggests
- accept invitations from other men
- never agree to sex until he has demonstrated that he wants more than just your body.

Of course, any of these responses could also mean exactly what it seems to: that she simply isn't interested. Nevertheless, though most men dislike the idea of being played like a fish, they quite admire women for having a seduction plan. It's more than they have.

When women talk, they tend to look each other in the eye. Men generally avoid eye-contact when talking to other men, thus doing away with the primitive need to lock horns and establish who is dominant. So if women are not interested, all they have to do is look away. The sign goes up: no vacancies.

Orgasms

Plant the thought in your listeners' minds that the next time they watch an urgent clash of flesh, or gasps of mutual ecstasy in a steamy Hollywood bonk-buster (good set of phrases, that – it'll recapture the attention of any drifters), they should remember that the average cinema-goer has an attention span of about 45 seconds. Even Sharon Stone confesses that she did women a disservice in *Basic Instinct* by suggesting that they could reach orgasm in about 30 seconds flat. This is just not how the female body works, and any woman who suggests other-wise is either a good actress, deluded or blessed by the gods.

For women, orgasm is not necessarily the goal. Physical intimacy, closeness, emotional bonding may give perfectly satisfactory sex. This is fortunate given that, according to the *Hite Report*, three-quarters of men ejaculate within two minutes of penetration. It is statements of this kind which lead women to believe the claim that: 'There is no such thing as a frigid woman; there is only an inadequate man.'

The male obsession with orgasm leads 50% of women to fake it in order to reassure their partner that he is not a failure – and nobody who has ever seen *When Harry Met Sally* can be in any doubt that women are supreme bluffers in this respect. Surveys also indicate that about the same number never reach a climax through intercourse. And 10% have never had one at all.

The problem is often that, for men, foreplay is a curtain-raiser whereas, for women, touching and stroking are a crucial part of the act (Acts I–V, if not the grand finale).

Men are charged with several million long-tailed gametes that are eager to get on with their job just as soon as optimum position for dispatch is achieved. This may be due to an instinctive fear. In the savannahs of Africa, a man might have been jumped on by a sabre-toothed tiger if he lingered too long. Unfortunately, it seems that the male body has not evolved in five million years to take account of the modern fashion for lingering – unless it's for sleep.

An added anxiety for women is the concept of the multiple orgasm. Men, with their competitive instincts, often feel the need to prove themselves good lovers by hammering away to try to bring this about, and many women feel that because the event is documented as attainable, they are failures if they don't themselves achieve it – even if their single orgasms rival Krakatoa.

Most women conclude at some point in their lives that the female body is badly designed. The clitoris, the main source of female orgasm, is a long way from centre stage; practically in the upper circle. Not the choicest place to guarantee stimulation during intercourse, especially in the man-on-top missionary position (which is probably why the killjoy missionaries recommended it). As with a dance tune, too often women only just begin to get the riff when the rhythm is over.

Men are frequently unaware that, though the source of women's pleasure may be the size of a peanut, it is armed with twice the sensitivity of a penis. This is a useful detail to keep ready. It is, you can say, the reason why the degree of delicacy in approaching such a minute hand-grenade can take years to get right. Diplomatically warn the men to whom you're bluffing that until that time arrives, many women would rather read a good book.

Contraception

In a survey, women were asked to cite the three most significant factors affecting female emancipation. They gave:

- the Pill
- the right to vote
- the washing machine.

Contraception liberates women to pursue the physical side of sex without feeling that they have to tie it to emotional commitment, though this does not mean that they will not also be on the lookout for that special person to whom they can make a long-term commitment. In other words, they can pursue sex in the way men have always done.

You can, of course, suggest that men have shown themselves willing to bear a greater responsibility for contraception, but be careful of mentioning the concept

of the male pill. This is something of a dead end. The
male pill has been shown to be effective, but even if
women could trust men to take it, the progesterone
(female hormone) content reduces the male sex-drive,
which rather defeats the object.

Promiscuity

If a man sleeps around he is considered a bit of a lad.
If a woman sleeps around she is considered a tramp.
Even women think so, although they may use a
gentler term such as 'slut'.

This disparity goes back to the primitive need of
men (even male gorillas) to be sure that the offspring
that they raise is their own and not someone else's. A
society dominated by males produces a patrilineal
system of inheritance, making it even more vital that
the father knows that his heirs are really his. Social
mores were formed around such patterns, and women
were probably too exhausted to argue.

In any case this attitude does not take account of
the philanthropic service performed by promiscuous
women in meeting the excessive need of men. There is
a phenomenon in the animal world – among apes and
elephants, for instance – known as the 'sneaky rutter'.
When the dominant male (read husband) is distracted,
a weaker rival male has a quick and surreptitious
fling with one of his females (read wife), who is usually
a willing party. A possible inference from this, you can
state drily, is that animals have an instinctive urge to
broaden the genetic pool. Then you should drop the
'dry' mask, pick up the one marked 'risqué', and add
that women who put themselves around might really
have the good of the human race at heart.

FEELINGS

Should discussion of the sexes' brains become too scientific, you may find it helpful in lightening the mood to mention the research that revealed that 'women use nine parts of their brain to get in touch with their feelings and men use only two – which they keep in their trousers'.

Guilt

It is rare to encounter bluffing material which you can use with an almost total guarantee that no-one will contradict you, but here we find such a statement: women feel guilty about everything, all the time. They feel guilty about their weight, their appearance, their careers, their mothering skills, the whiteness of their washes – even about dying. 'I don't mind dying, but it's leaving my man,' fretted Rose Rodin, the sculptor's wife. 'Who will look after him? What will happen to the poor thing?'

Above all, women feel guilty about not being perfect. They read articles in glossy magazines about 'having it all', padded with examples of Superwomen who effortlessly juggle high-flying careers, idyllic family lives, culinary triumphs, fashion-model figures and superb taste (with the help of a lot of money and an army of paid aid), and are racked with self-reproach for not managing it themselves (with the help of nobody).

Then they read articles about the folly of sacrificing quality of life and peace of mind to Superwoman ideals, and feel conscience-stricken about that too.

Luckily, women are ever-adaptable as well as ever-guilty. As Golda Meir robustly said when accused of neglecting her children (she was busy founding Israel at the time): 'You can get used to anything if you have to, even to feeling perpetually guilty.'

Just because you've taken this fact on board, do not fall into the trap that bluffer status will enable you to change it. A true bluffer always retains his or her humility. It is impossible to entice a women out of her guilt by either:

1. Encouragingly citing her strengths (it will only make her believe that anything you don't mention as a strength is a weakness).

2. Telling her she mustn't feel guilty (she will instantly assume she has something she hadn't even thought of yet to feel guilty about).

Saying Sorry

Men hate saying 'Sorry'. To them it's an admission of failure – or a confession that they have been found out. Women not only use the word to apologise, they also say 'Sorry' to express general sympathy and regret. (For example, her reaction to difficulties he may experience – being late because of traffic jams, getting drenched in the rain, his wife not understanding him – might elicit the response 'How awful for you... I'm so sorry.') Men's inability to grasp this distinction means that, when a woman says 'Sorry' to his tale of woe, he feels she has exonerated him from all blame.

Friendship

Friendship is enormously important to women – more important, indeed, than sex. It is also quite different for women than it is for men. Men want friends to play with (for example as golf partners, or as people with whom to go to the pub, watch the Cup Final and strip engines), whereas women want friends to talk to. Women have friends the way men have hobbies.

Ever since their far-off hunter-gathering days, the female instinct to socialise has remained so strong that it may well be regarded as the driving force behind human social behaviour. It is said that women are more interested in people, and men more interested in things – which goes some way towards explaining why men are rather better at mending cars than at small talk.

Women develop very close friendships with other women, often operating on intuitive understanding, as kindred spirits. Part of it is about using each other as sounding boards, sharing personal feelings, and being a psychiatric support group. A woman's female friends are also her network, her information service and her chief source of cultural and intellectual debate.

A curious phenomenon (and therefore something of maximum bluffing value) is that women are prepared to reorientate their social lives entirely towards a male partner in a manner not paralleled by men and their male pals. When a woman marries, and even more so when she starts to raise a family, her social horizons change and her old chums may drop, or be dropped, by the wayside in favour of new ones with similar concerns – and burdens.

Women would really like to be friends with men, but they can't get round the fact that most men won't indulge in free-range conversation – and to a woman, that's what friendship is all about. When they find a man who will chat about anything from communism to carpet shampoo, they stick to him like clingfilm because he is that rare creature who is able to dissociate himself from gender and talk about ideas.

Women want to fall in love with a man's mind – which isn't easy but explains why many form close friendships with homosexual men, who have the knack of being interested in the same things as women and, as one woman put it, 'at least will come shopping with you and offer an honest opinion'.

Strike a melancholy stance and offer the thought that the most fulfilling thing a woman can do is to feel really connected to another human being, whereas the most fulfilling thing a man can do is reach a climax. Sad really.

Motherhood

There is a mystique about motherhood which seems to assume that just because women can do it, all of them should want to.

Pregnancy can mean morning sickness, varicose veins, the physical shrinking of the brain, not to mention a craving for pickled onions and pawpaw. Any other condition that caused such symptoms would be under trial for a cure. It is no surprise that a fair number of women are not that keen.

Many women consider their role in reproduction to be nature's final act of vengeance against them – or even as definitive proof that God is a man. Why else, after the traumas of childbirth, would they gaze misty-eyed at a squalling bundle of dependency, and immediately, of their own free will, resolve to repeat the whole grisly experience?

It is a good thing that women are programmed to love their babies. Any other activity that caused sleepless nights and loss of free time would be avoided at all costs.

The urge to be a mother, if it visits at all, can hit the single woman just as forcefully as the woman who believes that she has found her life partner. Nowadays she can gratify it with the help of an anonymous donor. Scientists are apparently near to perfecting an artificial womb, which could help make the process less harrowing. Once that has been achieved, women could decide to eschew the physical process entirely by putting on a Brave New World-type production. A few choice male players might be kept, like prize bulls, in order to maintain supplies for the sperm bank.

It may be tempting, especially if you're bluffing in predominantly female company, to present this as a dream scenario. But we would caution against it. In reality women are not about to grab fertility and run. There may have been a radical shift in the ball park (as it were), but men are still required, and their services are appreciated. In any case, to hand child-birth over to a laboratory would be to hand over the trump card. And nothing will ever usurp the strange unfathomable sentiment that a woman can feel when she meets a man to whom she is instantly attracted and thinks: 'I want to have his children.'

In taking up this option you might suggest that women would be doing themselves a favour if they heeded the advice of one mother: 'Marry a man with a small head.'

Having a Good Cry

Although it is nowadays officially acceptable – even desirable – for men to cry, they will never be a match for women. Conditioned to stifle their emotions from birth, men will never understand how women can, in the right circumstances, claim to enjoy 'a good cry'.

One theory to which you can refer is that women may like a good cry at a weepie film because it gives them the catharsis of tears without the real emotional pain of their own lives. In other situations, tears are the physical release of pent-up emotions – not necessarily misery. Rage can precipitate women to tears more often than is generally imagined, and so can being happy.

Tears make men very uncomfortable, because they feel something is expected of them, but don't know what. Even women dither between tentative pats and strangled noises of sympathy or a crushing bear-hug.

Those caught in such situations can be reassured that in fact often no action is required; the tears are actually the solution.

ATTITUDES

To Men

'A woman need know but one man well in order to understand all men; whereas a man may know all women and understand not one of them,' wrote American journalist Helen Rowland in the 1920s.

It doesn't seem to bother men that women persistently make rude remarks about them, possibly because they are so used to it that they no longer really feel the barbs, or because they are so conceited they think women are joking. This is lucky, since women find very little to say in men's favour, and such plus points as they are prepared to concede tend to be grudging ('They're quite handy to have around') or condescending:

> Women's faults are many,
> Men have only two:
> Everything they say,
> And everything they do.

This may antagonise the men in your audience, but they are usually placated by being reminded that women constantly look for their good qualities: a sense of fair play, consideration for others, respect, a genuinely caring attitude, modesty, old-fashioned courtesy, and a sense of independence and individuality which is on the manageable side of psychotic. They seldom find them, however, and if they do, they cherish them like endangered species – which makes it easy for women gathered together and swapping anecdotes to end up feeling decidedly superior.

Confident of their own complexity, women just can't believe it possible that men are as transparent as they seem; that what you see is more or less all you get. 'The trouble with some women,' said Cher Bono, 'is they get all excited about nothing – and then marry him.' Women are convinced that somewhere in men must lurk a hidden store of untapped thoughts, insights and emotions, an inner self similar to their own, and that they only need find the key to unlock it. If a woman can find a way to a man's inner self she feels that precious sense of being the only one who knows him. She might, of course, be the only one who wants to.

Women find this search for the non-existent lode in men both frustrating and tantalising: men owe much of women's fascination with them to the false hope of its existence. This may be the most successful bluff on women they have ever achieved.

Yet whatever they may say, in practice women are remarkably tolerant of men. They are prepared to like them despite their failings; patiently bolster their egos knowing full well that men won't reciprocate, and give them the benefit of the doubt far beyond the point when doubt is a reasonable hypothesis.

However, whether they tolerate them, like them, or love them, women find men a constant disappointment. Even their own sons, apples of their eye, end up abandoning them for another woman.

The Drop Knickers Effect

There is a paucity of men whom women find irresistibly attractive, upon whom to unleash their passion. Men are notorious for being indiscriminate. Women are far more picky.

Men might take comfort from the fact that it is virtually impossible to predict which men will be judged by women to be attractive and which will be given the thumbs-down. Advertising companies play safe by veering between meticulous males with all-round appeal, and designer-stubbled scruffs, looking studiedly dissipated.

A survey conducted by a television game show found out what a woman first notices in a man. Top of the list, in order, were: eyes, bottom, clothes, cash, teeth, hair. Eyes, of course, are an important key to character. Bottoms are a feminine indulgence. Women find something very appealing about the shape of lean male buttocks, especially when tightly wrapped in a pair of jeans, and are fascinated by the way men have dents where women have bulges. It would, however, be a very foolish male who relied on this attribute alone for his appeal.

It will educate your male bluffees, while amusing the female ones, to point out that revealing all is not guaranteed to produce the ultimate sensation: on balance, more likely the opposite. As a female stripper teases her g-string, the males watch goggle-eyed, their salivating silence broken only by heavy breathing. Women watching a male stripper cheer and heckle raucously; they shriek with laughter. A gleaming, muscular male body is quite a treat, and sexy to boot, but it is also hugely funny. The question is, will he go all the way and produce the funniest thing of all? The naked truth is that women are more likely to be attracted to a man when he has his clothes on.

Impress people by revealing that if you ask any woman which male film stars make her go weak at the knees, which ones would make her throw husband, reputation and knickers to the wind, and the answer is extremely few: Donald Sutherland, Jean-Paul Belmondo (the *joli-laid* look), Sean Connery (worth mentioning in the company of bald men), Clint Eastwood (if wearing a poncho), Denzel Washington (leather trousers in *Much Ado About Nothing*), Brad Pitt, George Clooney (bedroom eyes), Cary Grant, Clark Gable (they don't have to be alive).

Harrison Ford does well – particularly that scene in the garage in *Witness* when he and the Amish woman look at each other, burning with illicit desire. Observe, as you remind your listeners of the scene, that Ford does not have to remove a stitch of clothing to achieve this.

Men may well become disheartened as the list of rejected Hollywood icons gets longer and longer, written off because they do not look trustworthy, fancy themselves too much, are too hairy, have no apparent intelligence, or lack strength of character. What hope is left for lesser mortals?

They needn't fret. Given the statistical chances of winning the man of their dreams, women usually settle for second best – which is where certain qualities come into play, such as good company, kindness, and clean fingernails. But the one quality which is guaranteed to win a woman's heart is a sense of humour. Lack of humour will often be cited as the Achilles heel of an otherwise desirable man.

Above all, women like men who show an interest in them. They can be as ugly as sin, but if they make a

woman feel important and cherished, if they can
amuse and entertain, the world is their oyster. The
18th-century reformer John Wilkes was notoriously
ugly, yet remarkably successful with women. 'I need
half an hour to talk away my face,' he explained.

In fact, it is a common occurrence for attractive
women to chose ugly men: they can be relied on not to
stray. This is possibly an instinctive throwback to the
days when it was important to keep a man close to
base when the babies started arriving, and it appears
to have some correlation in hormonal responses.
Austrian researchers have studied the effect of body
odour on stimulating attraction. Using T-shirts
impregnated with scent associated with attractive and
less attractive men, they gave these to women to sniff
throughout their menstrual cycle. They concluded that
women seemed more attracted to the scent associated
with the better looking men when at the beginning
and end of the cycle – but in the middle, when they
were at their most fertile, they were more attracted to
the uglier ones.

To Relationships

When men see an attractive woman, they fantasise
about sex. When women see an attractive man, they
fantasise about a relationship – charming, agreeable
company over dinner, friendship and comfort. Sex
does not necessarily come into it. What really matters
is two spirits enmeshed and invigorated by a magical
coalescence: this could be for ever. Most men are
blissfully unaware of this difference in attitude, or
refuse to believe it.

It is a mystery to women why men should be afraid
of commitment to a relationship, when long-term
relationships so patently benefit men more than

women. It is a known fact that divorced men die younger if they do not remarry.

Thanks to millennia of biological programming and their empathetic, social nature, most women want relationships, and are less afraid of committing to them than men – or, indeed, than is wise. They will settle for a good deal less than their fantasies: the occasional compliment, gift of flowers, dinner out or meal cooked for them, perhaps even a conversation, is enough to persuade a woman that she has found a truly caring man.

To Other Women

The biggest confidence trick ever played on women is the idea that other women are on their side. They aren't. Men may be the traditional enemy, but other women are the fifth column. Other women – unless they are family or friends, and sometimes not even then – are their rivals.

When a woman walks into a room at a business meeting or a party, another woman watching her may automatically think to herself, 'Is she prettier than me? Younger? Better dressed?'

It would be bad enough to appear unpresentable to a man, far worse before a group of women. Women have a knack of undermining each other and can do so with great precision. They insinuate criticism through apparent compliments, such as:

- 'You're looking very pretty tonight.' (You're usually so plain.)
- 'I always think that dress suits you so well.' (I see you're still wearing that old thing.)
- 'She always takes such trouble with her make-up.' (She needs to.)

To Daughters

Daughters are a threat to their mothers from the day they are born. Loved, indeed adored, on one level, they innocently arouse jealousy, irritation, envy, resentment and fury on another. Men do not understand the hostility which a mother can feel for her daughter just because the younger of the two has borrowed a 36D cup bra.

A wife might suggest to her husband that Wednesday would be a good night to go and see a new film but will be told he has too much work to do, his team is playing a championship match, or that romantic comedies are not his thing. Her daughter will then come along suggesting exactly the same thing and he will agree without hesitation. She can wind her father around her little finger.

Daughters, especially teenage daughters, are programmed to annoy their mothers beyond belief. It is a knack acquired early on that results in family scenes which always end in tears, recriminations, hugs and kisses and the mother giving her daughter whatever garment was stolen from her because she feels guilty for having been so mean. What seems to be forgotten during these episodes is that, once upon a time, the mother herself was a daughter.

To Marriage

'Bigamy is having one husband too many,' wrote Erica Jong, 'Monogamy is the same.' Men get a wife out of marriage: women get more work.

Nevertheless, getting married as opposed to being married – which is when women discover that 'happy ever after' is not quite the truth – remains an ideal objective for many women (or at least for their mothers). Having a Mateus Rosé wedding is the height of delight – floating across the meadow, in a white organza dress and dainty satin slippers, the groom moving towards her, his arms outstretched – this is the stuff of dreams.

Despite the harsh fact that in Britain one in three marriages now ends in divorce (one in two in the United States), people spend more on formal white weddings than ever before. Perhaps the more ostentatious and public the commitment, the more it is viewed as a talisman against divorce.

'It is a woman's business to get married as soon as possible,' mused George Bernard Shaw, 'and a man's to keep unmarried as long as he can.' Many women still feel that they haven't achieved their full potential unless they've netted a mate.

Their conditioning requires a male partner, but they know that they will have to coax, cajole and manipulate him into acting in anything approximate to his ideal role. The trouble is that men soon learn that their spouses are more expert at adapting, especially in relation to themselves. The uphill task of getting things done within marriage places women in four categories:

1. The woman who can do it and does it.

2. The woman who can do it, but waits for the man to do it for her.

3. The woman who, ever hopeful, says 'Darling, can you do it?' though she knows she's going to have to do it in the end.

4. The woman who has long since given up hope and doesn't even ask. She just does it.

In reality, what women need in marriage is a wife.

PRACTICALITIES

Coping

Women have a special aptitude for multi-tasking – i.e., managing several jobs or ideas at the same time. Men perform better at complicated linear problems, such as working out the trajectory of the football to the goal, but they usually cannot concentrate on anything else until they've done it. It takes a woman to load the washing machine while minding the baby, hearing the five-year-old's spellings, cooking dinner, planning tomorrow's wardrobe, creating a snappy slogan for her next multi-national marketing campaign, and deciding how to get her husband to ring his mother.

One of the key points about understanding women is the realisation that it isn't just that women can juggle several tasks at once – they are actually congenitally incapable of thinking of fewer than three things at a time. This is why so many female characters created by men seem implausibly two-dimensional. It may also be why more men than women commit suicide: the women are worrying that if they step off the world, the mince they left in the fridge will go off before it's eaten.

It is certainly why men are so often baffled by women's conversational leaps, and so blithely certain that whatever havoc men may cause, women will 'cope'. Women also secretly know they will cope, and even pride themselves on it. Coping is what women do.

Women at Work

More women than ever before are in paid employment, and in many ways the world of work has given in gracefully: maternity leave schemes, sexual harassment codes, flexi-time and crèches are now either statutory or are at least becoming widespread. Yet on average women still earn less than men for the same job, get fewer perks, and often hit an invisible yet tangible 'glass ceiling' halfway up the promotional ladder – only 11% of managers are women. Men find it hard to believe this barrier exists: 'I just don't see it,' they say, citing equal opportunities legislation. They wouldn't – it's glass.

For some time it was assumed that women, in order to succeed, had to behave like men – hiring and firing, confronting opposition head on and carving up rivals. These days the work culture is changing with the recognition that women's special aptitudes can bring identifiable business benefits. Women make work easier because they:

- are better at communicating
- are good at teamwork
- do umpteen things at once
- compromise without feeling any loss of face
- will make the coffee or take the minutes, provided it is made categorically clear that it isn't in their job description
- keep the grapevine going, along with the potted plants.

Yet statistics indicate that women still have to be considerably better than men to get the job offer. They can take comfort from the fact that, as Charlotte Whitton said when she was Mayor of Ottawa, 'Whatever women do they must do twice as well as men to be thought half as good. Luckily, this is not difficult.'

Depending on your bluffees' employment situations, you may like to suggest that, because women share Whitton's outlook, they prefer to work for a man than for another woman – men are easier to manipulate than women who have achieved success. Women know how tough it is, and are correspondingly hard on their underlings.

In spite of their inferior promotion prospects and remuneration, it has been found that women actually do more than men in the same job. It was a woman who pointed out that: 'Ginger Rogers could do everything Fred Astaire did, but in high heels.'

At work, all those things that fall into nobody's job description, such as putting more paper in the photocopier, checking there will be enough folders for the sales conference and explaining company policies to juniors, are done by women. A man may spend hours (of business time) writing memos about them, but it wouldn't occur to him to deal with them himself. One theory that bears some scrutiny is that women are not as status-ridden. But, by crossing demarcation lines as invisible to women as the glass ceiling is to men, women may inadvertently threaten the delicate, complex structure of power in men's highly politicised office world.

We would caution against citing examples of much-publicised female high-flyers: you are likely to get the retort that these are only newsworthy because they are still perceived as unusual. And when they fall, the press go into a kind of feeding frenzy, savage enough to leave male rivals feeling quite left out. Women in politics are singled out for particularly thorough scrutiny. Should they turn out to have a voice of their own, to give as good as they get in the combative atmosphere of active government, they are quickly labelled brusque, sharp-tongued, a termagant. It takes a male politician years of haranguing and carping to achieve this kind of reputation.

What is it then that keeps women trying to batter down the doors to the last few uncongenial bastions of male domination – sewerage maintenance, army boot camps, Mount Athos? Should you be called upon to answer this query, suggest that it's the same compulsion that makes small children put beans in their ears: the fact that they have been warned off lends allure. Besides, some male bastions have proved worth besieging in the past. And women have an irresistible urge to try them all out for size.

Housework

These days, men can and do cook, iron and vacuum, and have even been known to clean the bath. But surveys show that women still spend four to five times as long on domestic chores as their helpful husbands.

Men tend to see housework as an option, a special extra job they do to demonstrate how modern they are: they are genuinely baffled by the fury it can rouse in a woman if they innocently ask 'Can I help?' Wives don't want husbands to help: they want them to recognise that they bear equal responsibility for running the household.

The fact is that men can tolerate a greater degree of grime and disorder than women before they even notice it, so it is usually the woman who heads for the broom cupboard first. Happily, this does at least pay off in property values: when couples sell their separate flats to buy a house together, in 90% of cases it is the woman's that sells first.

Map-Reading

Because many women will turn maps upside down so the roads drawn match their direction of travel, they are often assumed to be useless map-readers. Yet in other circumstances, such as peeking at memos across desks, reading upside down is regarded as clever.

Some women really do have trouble map-reading, as do some men. But being curious, women also want to be watching what is going on outside the windows instead of staring fixedly at the atlas on their knees, which everyone knows makes you carsick. Researchers at the Ruhr University in Germany have found that oestrogen interferes with 'spacial intelligence'. So if you want a woman to navigate, recruit her during her period when oestrogen levels are lower.

Many women have overcome their disadvantages to become perfectly competent navigators. They are often hampered, however, by male drivers who refuse to believe they really do mean 'Turn left', ignore the instruction, or argue that straight on must be quicker.

Punctuality

There are people of both genders who are congenitally poor timekeepers, but, these menaces aside, women are in fact rarely unpunctual. And if they are, they didn't mean to be.

There is a fundamental misunderstanding between the sexes over what punctuality is. Men, with their more linear thought processes, and a certain degree of selfishness, want to get on with the next item on their agenda as soon as they reach it. Women, being more flexible in their approach and needing to incorporate all sorts of diversions en route – dropping off the dry cleaning, picking up the children, returning the library books, waiting for the wheel-clamp removers – find that time just doesn't stretch the way it should.

Many women also deliberately arrive ten minutes after the time agreed, to avoid the risk of waiting alone in a wine bar, restaurant or, worse, on a street corner because of... men.

FOIBLES

Intuition

Women take great pride in their intuition. They find it hard to accept that men are not armed with the same sense of instinctive insight – and are consistently let down by this. It is the basis of one of the key areas of misunderstanding between the sexes.

Men usually fail to notice if anyone has a problem until it is either brought to their notice or has become too obvious to ignore. They then presume that resolution lies in immediately proposing solutions. Men like to appear decisive. Women tend to pre-empt acutely problematic situations, thanks to their well-developed antennae.

'A woman's guess is much more accurate than a man's certainty,' wrote Rudyard Kipling; and even sour William Hazlitt grudgingly acknowledged that 'Women never reason, and therefore they are (comparatively) seldom wrong'.

Women listen more intently, and are capable of picking up other people's moods and feelings by reading infinitesimal signs on their faces, in their eyes, or in their movements. They can sense in an instant if something is not right – a flash of a glance or a hesitancy which conceals an untruth.

Much of women's intuition can be explained by the mental and social ways they operate. Women are genuinely interested in people, and spend a lot of time working out what makes them tick. Thus what may seem like a snap character assessment may well be based on reasoning, proceeding from particular cases to general conclusions, which is a scientifically respectable principle of analysis. They will diagnose someone's lifestyle from the contents of their supermarket trolley, i.e., several children, a teenage vegetarian, three dogs, and an overweight husband with irregular motions and a potting shed.

Many men profess to be completely baffled by the way women can leap from speculation to certainty without due process of deduction between the two. Women are largely indulgent of this male bafflement, partly because it's no more than they expect, and partly because it gives them the upper hand.

Going to the Lavatory in Pairs

If men got up in pairs to go to the lavatory, their relationship would immediately come under question. Yet women do it all the time, and nobody reads anything into it. Nor is it the case that the one who said 'I'll come with you' had been crossing her legs for hours, but was too shy to mention her need in mixed company.

This tribal rite is possibly the most asked-about feature of women's behaviour. Consequently, to keep your bluffer's nose in front of the competition, you should have a variety of answers on which you can draw:

- Women seek safety in numbers.
- They want to get together to exchange confidences.
- They don't trust the other woman enough to leave her alone with the men, so they encourage her to come too.
- They don't want to use the lavatory at all, just the mirror to check their make-up.

Basically, nobody really understands women's reasons for communal comfort stops. It could be an extension of the female propensity to match each other's hormonal rhythms, or just that they are naturally sociable. As the Irish say, 'Will you walk with me to take the bare look off me?'

Gossip

Gossip is an essential component of women's friendships, and not at all the character assassination men often seem to think it is. As American broadcaster Barbara Walters said: 'Show me someone who never gossips, and I'll show you someone who isn't interested in people.'

If the venue for your bluffing is a party, you can have a lot of fun (and thereby your enhance your all-knowing image) by asking a woman for a description of a recently-departed guest. You will be sure to get the full identikit from height and figure to good teeth and plucked eyebrows. Then ask a man who has not heard the woman's answer. You will probably get: 'I didn't really notice. I only saw her legs.'

'But what were you talking about?' a bemused man may ask a woman who has just spent two hours on the phone to someone she saw only that morning, or is just setting off to meet. In general, men regard conversation strictly as a means of imparting essential information; they don't understand that, to women, all information is essential, and gossip is therefore the vital currency of life.

Revenge

A trusty stalwart in the bluffer's armoury, useful if the discussion has become a little staid, revenge gives you the excuse to refer to those juicy tabloid tales of that fiercest of creatures, the woman scorned. Every now and then she reaches the front page for carving up her ex-husband's entire wardrobe, for throwing bleach over his Lamborghini, or for attempting to ensure that no other woman will enjoy the pleasure of his most intimate assets.

Your underlying thesis for this behaviour should be one of emotional investment. If a man has been scorned, he would rather pretend it hasn't happened. A scorned woman is engulfed by loss: she may have given the best years of her life to that man, her youthful looks, her fertility. She has learnt to know him better than he knows himself, and made untold compromises to accommodate him. She could forgive him everything he did while he was still with her, but nothing once he has gone. Above all, she cannot forgive him for no longer finding her desirable.

It is painful enough to face the fact that he has exchanged her for a younger model – but even more distressing that he is treated with understanding, sympathy, even admiration by everyone else. Being abandoned is a desperately lonely business. Few seem willing to join the scorned woman in building the pyre and hammering in the stake to which her ex deserves to be lashed.

So it is no surprise that she feels vengeful, and expresses this with her own brand of urban guerilla tactics, such as connecting the telephone to a talking timetable in Brazil, dampening a carpet and sowing it with cress seeds, or hiding fish heads behind the dashboard. She may feel that TV's Roseanne Barr had it just about right when she said: 'I'm not upset at getting divorced, but I'd rather be a widow.'

Nagging

Should this word crop up in conversation, we suggest you offer the opinion that a woman does not nag, she reminds. This point cannot be made too often. It is a fact that should be underlined several times over, at regular intervals throughout the day, and pinned to the kitchen noticeboard. Women do not nag.

Even if someone is under the impression that a woman is nagging, going on and on about something, she is not actually nagging, but reminding, and it is probably for their own good. There is absolutely no point in considering the matter any further until they have taken this idea on board.

Nagging, you should maintain, is not a female characteristic; this is a misapprehension put about by hen-pecked husbands who should know better. They are simply being apprised of the fact that they have not done what they said they were going to do, and need to be prompted, regularly, otherwise it won't get done.

Besides, once men realise that they can rely on women to remind them of the simple things that would otherwise clutter their minds, they come to depend on it. So they need to be reminded. Regularly.

Cattiness

Women believe they can get away with the sort of remarks that get men shot down in flames. Being catty is deemed a noble pursuit, like duelling. At its best its rapier precision can win the admiration, respect and terror of both sexes. 'Boy George is all Britain needs,' declared Joan Rivers. 'Another queen who can't dress.'

Their excuse for this behaviour is that for cent·ries they were physically, legally and socially dependent on men whom they had to flatter and beguile at every turn for fear of being abandoned, so they had no other means to assert themselves besides denigrating men, or other women who might usurp them. In fact, like cats, they just have this savage streak which they are quite unable to control.

But generally cattiness is more about mockery and

teasing than aggression. Women tend to look wryly at life from the underside – it's the view they're most used to. Dorothy Parker was an expert practitioner: when told that rival journalist Clare Booth Luce was invariably kind to her inferiors she asked, 'And where does she find them?'

The truly deft catty remark can often contain a nugget of universal truth, e.g: 'The trouble with Jane is that she's still young enough to think that one man may be better than another.'

Shopping

Though many women actually dislike shopping, the fact remains that by and large women shop in a way few men do. It certainly isn't about acquiring material possessions: a dedicated female shopper can come back as happy from an all-day expedition with no purchases as with a lorryload. On the other hand, just buying a lipstick can give her a kick.

The point to focus on here, is that shopping can stimulate endorphins (the body's own morphia) which temporarily promotes a feel-good factor and, like chocolate, it can quickly become addictive.

Appearance

The first thing a woman thinks of when asked to go somewhere is 'What am I going to wear?'

In a truly egalitarian society women would take as much trouble to dress as many men. That is to say, they would frequently sport dirty hair, and recycle crumpled clothes from the laundry basket when they ran out of clean ones.

Or perhaps not. Presentation is important to women.

Their clothes serve as a pick-me-up on down days or as a suit of armour from inside which they can confidently outface a hostile world. However, deciding upon the right outfit – the one that brings a glint of approval or, even better, a gleam of envy to another woman's eyes – is a cause for anxiety. How to find the outfit that proclaims the wearer to be simultaneously fashionable, at ease with her body, and successfully in control of her life?

A good example is the casual lunch party where the hostess insists that guests must 'come as you are'. The men will take this literally, and make an uninterrupted journey from under the car to the hostess's door in oil-smeared jeans and a holey jersey with dead leaves still stuck to it. 'Leave me alone,' he will insist when his wife tries to dust him off as they walk up the garden path. 'She said "come as you are", didn't she?'

His wife will have her own very different interpretation of this dress code which will represent, minimally, the third set of clothes she tried on that morning.

Men would be wise not to question this. Women love dressing up; they love to have an occasion to put on their glad rags, especially if the occasion demands a hat. But, more and more, they have come to realise the benefits of dressing like a man; discovered the liberation that proceeds not only from the bliss of covering defects under dateless trousers and jacket, but also from eliminating the time and stress usually involved with choice.

The more women assume an outwardly take-me-seriously, unfussy style of clothing, the happier they are to indulge in frivolities underneath. As they did not wear knickers at all until the Victorian era, they could be making up for lost time. However, being given bright red silk lingerie for Valentine's Day might invite the question: 'Is this your present, or mine?'

Pretty Woman

To men, and to most women as well, it can seem that life is a breeze for a pretty woman. Doors open for her that remain firmly closed for the rest when she walks into a room, sullen men sparkle, rich potential husbands jump out of the woodwork, the whole world seems brighter and sexier and more like a spread from *Hello!* magazine. She is even able to earn 10% more than plainer female counterparts.

In fact, good looks can be a terrible blight. Most men will not be able to talk to pretty women without having 'fwaw! she's gorgeous!' written all over their faces. Most women will look at pretty women with steely eyes.

Psychologists in Italy who monitored the attention levels of 1,500 males watching the news discovered that when it was presented by an attractive female, three-quarters of them failed to absorb 60% of what was said. On the other hand, if the news reader was considered unattractive, only 28% passed over their heads.

Another difficulty arises: men appear to find it hard to believe that a woman can be both beautiful and intelligent – 'not just a pretty face'. They can become so taken with the gift-wrapping that it doesn't occur to them there might be real gifts inside. Thus in business, prettiness can be as much a disadvantage to an intelligent woman as being plain can be to anyone else.

Then there is the question of ageing: a pretty woman may define herself by her looks, so what is left when it fades?

However some pretty women manage to sail through in triumph, skilled and intelligent enough to be grateful for nature's gifts, and able to handle the pitfalls. And all young girls still want to grow up to be pretty.

Dieting

Very few women conform to the perceived ideal for the female shape, and virtually all of them worry about it. Surveys are disturbing. For instance, it has been found that in job interviews women with a low 'hip-to-waist' ratio are more likely to succeed. In other words they look more male. The editor of *Yes!* (a magazine for larger women) puts it brutally: 'It isn't true and it isn't fair, but ultimately curvaceous women are seen as stupid, lazy, and greedy.'

Faced with this topic, you can adopt one of two strategies. If you wish to bluff against the tide a little, you can refer to two other surveys revealing that women with narrower hips also have higher testosterone levels – and so do violent female offenders.

But if you feel it easier to go with the flow, your opening remark (delivered with a 'tant pis' air) should be that no constructive comment will stop a woman who is discontented with her body shape from dieting. Over 50% of Western women are on a diet at any one time. Women diet despite the well-publicised fact that dieting doesn't work. They do not do so simply to achieve the optimum weight for their figure and health. They diet because they secretly hope (even though they know it isn't true) that eating a lunchtime rusk which tastes about as good as its box will turn a Dolly Parton shape into a Kate Moss one. And that this will make them happy.

You could then move on from this expression of regret to make derogatory remarks about 'the body fascists' – the fashion, advertising and health industries. Alternatively, talk dreamily of other eras. The Venus de Milo is a BIG woman. Marilyn Monroe was decidedly voluptuous by today's standards. Not only will this forge bonds with your female bluffees, it will bring a lustful glint to the eyes of your male ones.

Feminine Wiles

Little girls charm their fathers into a suspension of rational thought. Teenage girls plot every move they make. Married women give their husbands as much rope as they think is necessary for them to swing back to their way of thinking. But women deny that they operate anything as nebulous and sinister as 'wiles'. These are legitimate tactics.

SENSITIVE SUBJECTS

Intelligence

'A woman who has the misfortune of knowing anything,' wrote the 19th-century novelist Frances Trollope, 'should conceal it as well as she can.'

It is a sad truth that while men can stomach sparkles of intelligence from a woman, they find too much intellect indigestible. Intelligent women are a threat, and women have to take this into account if they wish to make headway with men. Men need to feel they are superior in the brainpower department. Women have to waste considerable amounts of their ingenuity and wit pretending that this is the case. It was a man who ruefully admitted: 'Women are more intelligent than men. They have to be, to convince us so often that the opposite is true.'

As an added complication, most women genuinely want their partner to be their intellectual superior: in any random survey, they will identify the man as the more intelligent of the partnership (as, of course, will the men).

The game was largely blown open by the Women's Lib movement and subsequent research into gender-comparative intelligence. It became an inescapable, official, scientific fact that all other things being equal, women are in general more intelligent. However, women still consistently underrate their I.Q.s, while men consistently overrate theirs. This oddity is encapsulated by Anita Loos' complaint: 'The people I'm furious with are the women's liberationalists. They keep getting on soapboxes and proclaiming women are brighter than men. That's true, but it should be kept quiet or it ruins the whole racket.'

A Rose by Any Other Name

Women do not have a one-size-fits-all label to hang around their neck. 'Woman' sounds slightly biological and mature – not a word that a 16-year-old would readily apply to herself. 'Girl' carries a hard-to-define sell-by date; warn your audience that it is generally accepted as unsuitable for any female over the age of eleven. However, women of a certain age are permitted to use it of themselves and their chums, as in works' canteens, golf clubs and 'girls' night out'. 'Ladies' is for W.C.s, women in big hats, and women who are clearly anything but. One solution, widespread in America and Australia, is to use the word 'guys' irrespective of gender.

It is a constant source of annoyance to large numbers of women that their marital status has to be broadcast by the titles Miss and Mrs. They feel it should be nobody's business but their own. Besides, with more women keeping their own surname after marriage, it can be tricky to decide which title applies: as married women they are no longer Miss, but they are not Mrs. Maiden Name either.

Ms. has become the generally accepted compromise, but unfortunately no-one knows how to pronounce it without a faint sneer.

Feminism

We strongly urge you to expunge from your bluffing any assumption that feminism has now become old hat, as outmoded as a hatpin or a mink stole with the head still on. It may lead you into dangerous territory, for along the way strewn with burnt bras there are plenty of embers which can easily be fanned into a fire. The truth is that many women still feel hard done by, and there are lots of statistics to show that they get a raw deal. The women's movement was propelled forward by the French Revolution, the struggle for the emancipation of slaves, and votes for women, and plenty of women believe that there are more shackles to be torn asunder and that more heads should roll before the feminist goal of equality is reached.

At the base of feminism is a fundamental injustice, still unresolved. Elena Gianini Belotti put it in a nutshell when she wrote: 'No woman, except for so-called deviants, seriously wishes to be male and have a penis. But most women would like to have the privileges and opportunities that go with it.'

Feminism can be presented as a two-edged sword for a great many women are starting to miss the little courtesies that were once ingrained in men. There is a sad truth in the tale that is brought out whenever men are accused of lack of politesse: 'I offered my seat to a woman once and she turned out to be a feminist and shouted at me, so I'm afraid of doing it again.' Someone must find this feminist harridan and stop her.

Women Drivers

There is a universal assumption that women and machines are simply incompatible. In fact it is really a question of attitude. Women do not wish to spend their Sunday afternoons dismantling their carburettor because:

a) there are people they can pay to do that for them, and

b) there are better things to do.

Society seems to have an in-built prejudice about this. It is perfectly acceptable for a man to say that he cannot make head nor tail of the instructions for some mobile phone in a literal translation from Taiwanese; if a woman does the same, it is greeted by men with deep sighs and derision.

'Woman driver' is an insult generally flung by a man at a woman who drives like he does. But 90% of speeding convictions and 94% of accidents involve men, and insurance companies have responded by offering lower rates to women, as a better risk.

The assumption that women have no idea of what happens under the bonnet is also suspect: from sheer self-preservation, most women know how to spray spark plugs and change a tyre – but would rather pretend ignorance so as not to get oily.

Computers and videos come into the same category. It is true that more men than women explore the full potential of their computers, and that 85% of Internet users are men – but around the same percentage applies to the denizens of amusement arcades.

Many people are aware that Charles Babbage invented the first computer (almost all inventors are men; women would rather solve the problems they already have), but bluffers can make the point that it was a woman, Countess Ada Lovelace (daughter of

Byron) who programmed it for him. And another, Commander Grace Hopper of the U.S. Navy, who invented the programming language COBOL in the 1950s and, possibly more usefully in the electronic world, the term 'bug'.

Being Single

Unlike 'bachelor', the word 'spinster' implies a crabby, lonely old age in a room ridden with cats and knick-knacks. Most single women prefer the term 'single woman' which they feel carries quite different connotations – debonair, carefree, and rather clever to have evaded the mundane chores of marriage. But after 30, they may be viewed as either unnecessarily self-sufficient or rather daring (provided that they do not exude an air of quiet desperation).

To married men a single woman is a wasted asset. To women she is a loose cannon. The comment 'She's never been married', usually made by married women to each other, is a form of put-down. For some, the single woman rests in limbo, her state and status similar to uncooked dough. Marriage is the oven of social pairing – living together is the microwave. Mere cohabiting is ruled out of this equation: she has not nailed her man.

Newsweek came up with the statistic that a college-educated woman of 30 had only a 20% chance of ever marrying; at 40, she had more chance of being murdered by a terrorist than finding a husband.

Despite the male fear of commitment, a random survey of people over 30 reveals that the vast majority of really bright men are married, and the vast majority of single women are really bright. Speculating about this in the company of married women requires care, but is nearly always successful with single ones.

Divorcees, by contrast, are seen as powerful – the mere fact of having been married proves they can fulfil woman's traditional role, and they are thereby freed to fulfil others. They have been there, done that, and come out stronger than ever on the other side.

Novelist Marie Corelli summed up her single state like this: 'I never married because there was no need. I have three pets at home which answer the same purpose as a husband. I have a dog which growls every morning, a parrot which swears all the afternoon, and a cat that comes home late at night.'

P.M.T./P.M.S.

Women claim that they got dumped with periods because men couldn't take them. Not for nothing is it called 'the curse': periods are painful, smelly, messy and generally irksome. The only way to avoid menstruation is by becoming pregnant: out of the frying pan and into the fire.

Women's moods are controlled by this monthly cycle. Strange things happen to them as their period approaches – the phenomenon known as P.M.T. At least 50% of women say they suffer from it, and 5-10% to a debilitating degree. On their personal Richter scale, they may register anything from tremors of irritability to earth-shaking rages. (Why does it take six P.M.T. women to change a light bulb? *Because it just DOES!!!*)

Tempers are not improved by the fact that they feel themselves to be distracted, clumsy, weepy, and heavier by several pounds. They may also get more interested in sex.

These days, there are endless products designed to make menstruation less burdensome – and from the advertisements, an unknowing man or child might assume that it was a time of unusual exuberance and flights of joy, accompanied by blue emissions. Periods can be a trump card or a joker – a reassuring sign for some that they are not pregnant, devastating proof for others that they have yet again failed to conceive. Some women claim that their periods give them a sense of cyclical renewal, of physical cleansing. They may even remember their first period as a mystical experience that confirmed their entry into womanhood. But be careful; treat this as a passive component of your bluffing, one to be empathised with should a female listener volunteer it, not one that you should raise yourself. Force it on a woman who happens to be one of the 'debilitating degree' percentage and anything could happen.

Menopause

Women's attitude to the menopause is ambivalent. The natural cessation of fertility may have come in the past as a blessed relief to some but, today, women tend to regard it less as an end to problems associated with their periods, and more as an indication of new problems to come.

The diminution of female oestrogen is not, alas, an overnight process. It can involve:

- fatigue
- hot flushes or 'power surges'
- the onset of chin hair (associated with testosterone previously held in equilibrium by the oestrogen) – inexplicable emotional outbursts
- night sweats
- loss of concentration of the kind that leads to buttering the cork mats instead of the toast.

To counteract this barrelful of woe, many women use Hormone Replacement Therapy (H.R.T.), which effectively fools the body by replacing the lost oestrogen. (The Japanese who have the highest consumption of plant oestrogens, found in soya flour and linseed oil, have no word for the menopause.)

Humans are among the very rare animals to cease fertility in this way. It has been suggested that it serves a useful evolutionary function: women stop being burdened by having babies at a time when their own daughters are starting to produce them. This allows them to concentrate on handing down knowledge about breast feeding, potty-training, the best recipe for rabbit pie, the social acceptability of fish knives, and other tribal traditions.

In the company of women, it is probably a good idea to avoid any suggestion that there is an equivalent 'male menopause'; most women will greet it with hoots of derision. They see this at best as an honorary title for the mid-life crisis, and certainly not entailing an equivalent physical or emotional see-saw.

Women can also have mid-life crises when they realise that they haven't had a life and are already half way through it. The idealism of youth may have vanished, but there may still be a last chance for fulfilment. This recognition hits women about ten years earlier than men – around the age of 35. As it happens, 35 is, for women, the average age for divorce.

Vulnerability

Women suffer from a deep sense of vulnerability. Part of this is purely physical – the fear of being raped, assaulted or just put upon by someone physically stronger and infinitely more aggressive. (In the U.S., 85% of violent crime is committed by men. The 15%

committed by women may seem surprisingly high, but it includes domestic spats: when women murder, they usually kill someone they know.)

Fear defines a woman's freedom. She is simply unable to move around the world with the liberty of a man. A lone male hitchhiker is adventurous, a lone female one is 'looking for trouble'. Even in her own immediate neighbourhood she is subconsciously aware of the need to remain streetwise, check she is not being followed, be ever ready to flee or ask for help.

When a judge let a rapist go free because his mini-skirted victim had been 'asking for it', the American writer Ellen Cleghorn wryly remarked that the next time women saw an ugly man on the street they should shoot him: 'After all, he knew he was ugly when he left the house. He was asking for it.'

Ageing

Women and age are not compatible. Ageing becomes a serious issue after the age of about 29; after that age women become wary of full-length mirrors. This is an extremely touchy subject and should be treated with extreme caution. Mention the 'biological clock' at your peril: it is wired to a time bomb.

A woman 'of a certain age' is still very reluctant to reveal it. The general view seems to be that she should pick a good age and stick with it, even if it technically illegitimises her offspring. Lying about age is a skill: it needs a facility for maths in order to calculate the year one was supposed to have been born, and care to ensure one did not start work at the tender age of ten. (Yet the pendulum swings completely when a woman gets to 'a grand old age', and proudly announces that she is in her 79th/89th/99th year just to bask in the gasps of astonishment.)

121

Men reach the height of their fertility at around the age of 15, which in the case of a fair number of them happens to coincide with the end of their mental development. Women reach the height of their fertility in two waves, in the late teens, and again in their late thirties. This gives rise to a parallel paradox: at 15, girls do their utmost to look as though they are 35; when they are 35 they try in vain to look 15.

Women will make huge efforts to disguise the visible signs of ageing – dyeing their hair, slapping on creams, injecting fat into parts of their body which age has made thin and taking it out of parts grown too fat, and in extreme cases undergoing plastic surgery by winding in the whole skin covering like a sardine lid.

The real enemy is gravity: it makes women sag. If you are bluffing on the move – a bus or a train – cast a discrete eye around for any woman seated with a stiff back and a rictus grin on her face. Then, maintaining subtlety as your byword, alert your bluffee to this woman explaining that she is probably engaged in pelvic floor exercises, designed to counteract the wearing effect of gravity on her internal organs.

The same gravitational effect on breasts is receiving attention from a group of aviation engineers who are working on designs for a truly effective bra. According to them, the problems of support for front-loaded mammary glands and engines mounted on the underside of aeroplane wings are, in engineering terms, identical.

THINGS WOMEN SHOULD TELL OTHER WOMEN ABOUT MEN

Dogs are more rewarding than men because.

You can house train a dog.

Dogs at least attempt to find what they've mislaid before appealing to you.

Middle-aged dogs don't feel the need to abandon you for a younger owner.

* * *

Men are like mascara. They usually run at the first sign of emotion.

The best way to get a man to do something is to suggest he is too old for it.

A man marries a woman expecting that she won't change, but she does. A woman marries a man expecting that he will change, but he doesn't.

Men seldom make passes at a girl who surpasses.

His having a sense of humour does not mean that he laughs at your jokes. It means that you laugh at his.

A man's got to do what a man's got to do. A woman must do what he can't.

* * *

Men are like computers because:

In order to get their attention, you have to turn them on.

Big power surges knock them out for the rest of the night.

GLOSSARY

Ardent feminist – Woman whose real venom is reserved for women who take a different standpoint from her own.

Bachelor – A man who has missed the opportunity to make some woman miserable.

Bra – An over shoulder boulder holder.

Breasts – Source of food for babies and fascination for men, also known as balloons, baps, bazoomas, boobs, bosoms, Bristols, bubs, bust, chubbies, dugs, fun bags, globes, grapefruits, kazongas, knockers, jugs, melons, tits, twin peaks, upper deck, wongas.

Childbirth – An experience likened to having one's lower lip pulled right up over one's head.

Clitoris – Female sex organ: the only bit of the human body (male or female) which appears to have no other function besides pleasure.

Doormat – Woman who allows her husband to wipe his feet on her, then shakes the mat outside and squares it off neatly.

Foreplay – Something men play at a few minutes before.

Friend – Bosom pal.

Housework – Work that can all be destroyed half an hour after you've done it. And no-one notices that you've done it but everyone notices if you haven't.

Husband – Man who before marriage knows where his things are, and after it, doesn't.

Man's woman – Female with an inbuilt tracking device for seeking out the nearest male.

Menopause – Rather more than a pause between men.

Mother-in-law – The 'other woman' in a wife's life.

Oestrogen (spelt estrogen in the U.S. and pronounced Eee-strogen in the U.K.) – The defining female hormone, also found in men.

PMT/PMS – Pre-menstrual tension (syndrome in the U.S., where everything is bigger). If you do not know what it is, try suggesting to a woman who has it that it's a figment of her imagination.

Pubic hair – The most visible aspect of female genitalia, a.k.a. bush, beaver, muff, Taz (Australian, after the shape of Tasmania), and according to some etymologists the origin of the word nitty-gritty.

Testosterone – The defining male hormone, also found in women. Responsible for aggressive behaviour, hairiness and 'top-shelf' publications.

Tramp – Woman who distributes her favours too liberally, a.k.a. bicycle, easy lay, jumper, slapper, scrubber, shag bag, tart (originally a diminutive of sweetheart).

Vagina/vulva – The passage through which all human life traditionally has passed, a.k.a. clunge, cockpit, conch, crack, cush, fanny (not in U.S.), front bottom, wick burner, happy valley, honey pot, prat, privy seal, pudenda, pussy, quim, tail, twat. There is also the hateful c.... word.

THE AUTHORS

Antony Mason is the author of some 40 books on travel, exploration, history, geography, spying, volleyball, house plants, the Belgians... In other words, he is a consummate bluffer, though he would not put it like that, publicly at least.

Like most males, as a boy he was constantly urged to be a man. Now that he is one, he realises that this is one of the world's greatest bluffs. Although well into his forties, if separated from a mirror he imagines he is about 18, and certainly wishes he was – were it possible to do without all those sticky agonies of adolescence. 'Forty-something going on fourteen,' says his wife. But then women think they know all about men – a prejudice that the author would like to shoot down with all guns blazing. Neeeeorrrrrr! Dat dat dat dat dat dat!

Marina Muratore is a child-care officer with years of experience working in nurseries in the public sector, a career which she feels has afforded her unique insight into the differences between men and women.

She is married to writer Antony Mason, author of *The Bluffer's® Guide to Men*. He sits upstairs, locked away with his important work, while she does the ironing and prepares the children's tea – for the child in the garden and the one upstairs.

Collaboration on *The Bluffer's® Guide to Women* has given Marina the chance to get even. Never before had they looked at men and women so thoroughly and so candidly – at least in each other's company. For her husband this process served to increase the fascinating mystery and mystique of women. For her, men became even more comprehensible, not to say transparent. As it happens, these were approximately the same relative positions that they started with.

THE BLUFFER'S® GUIDES

The three million-copy best-selling humour series that contains facts, jargon and inside information – all you need to know to hold your own among experts.

Accountancy
Astrology & Fortune
  Telling
Archaeology
Ballet
The Classics
Chess
Computers
Consultancy
Cricket
Doctoring
Economics
The Flight Deck
Football
Golf
The Internet
Jazz
Law
Management
Marketing
Men
Middle Age
Music

Opera
Personal Finance
Philosophy
Public Speaking
The Quantum
  Universe
Relationships
The Rock Business
Rugby
Science
Secretaries
Seduction
Sex
Skiing
Small Business
Stocks & Shares
Tax
Teaching
University
Whisky
Wine
Women